SOUTH
AMERICAN
GRILL

SOUTH AMERICAN GRILL

RACHAEL LANE

hardie grant books

MELBOURNE · LONDON

PUBLISHED IN 2012 BY HARDIE GRANT BOOKS

HARDIE GRANT BOOKS (AUSTRALIA)   HARDIE GRANT BOOKS (UK)
GROUND FLOOR, BUILDING 1   DUDLEY HOUSE, NORTH SUITE
658 CHURCH STREET   34–35 SOUTHAMPTON STREET
RICHMOND, VICTORIA 3121   LONDON WC2E 7HF
WWW.HARDIEGRANT.COM.AU   WWW.HARDIEGRANT.CO.UK

CATALOGUING-IN-PUBLICATION DATA IS AVAILABLE FROM THE NATIONAL LIBRARY OF AUSTRALIA.
SOUTH AMERICAN GRILL
ISBN 9 781742703008

PUBLISHING DIRECTOR: PAUL MCNALLY
PROJECT EDITOR: LUCY HEAVER
EDITOR: JACQUELINE BLANCHARD
DESIGN MANAGER: HEATHER MENZIES
DESIGNER: JAY RYVES, FUTURE CLASSIC
PHOTOGRAPHER: BONNIE SAVAGE
STYLIST: LEE BLAYLOCK
LANGUAGE CONSULTANT: ANA GABRIELA AMADOR
PRODUCTION: PENNY SANDERSON

COLOUR REPRODUCTION BY SPLITTING IMAGE COLOUR STUDIO
PRINTED AND BOUND IN CHINA BY 1010 PRINTING INTERNATIONAL LIMITED

CONTENTS

INTRODUCTION

South American–style grilling is a carnivore's delight. The barbecue tradition of South America originated on the fertile plains of Southern Brazil, Argentina, Patagonia (Southern Chile), Paraguay and Uruguay, where traditional cattlemen, known as *gauchos*, would herd their livestock. The *gauchos* would build large pit fires and cook whole carcasses splayed out on metal crosses and smaller pieces of meat skewered onto their knives over the remaining hot coals. The meat was seasoned with little more than some salt and perhaps a few herbs that they had collected along the way.

The flavours of South American food are as vibrant and varied as its people and landscape. Each country has its own unique native dishes as well as those that have developed and evolved from the food traditions brought to them by early colonisers, slaves and immigrants. The blending of native ingredients along with those imported and introduced from distant lands have created the myriad of spicy flavours indicative of South American cuisine and have helped shape the food culture to become what it is today.

These traditional styles of grilling are known as *asado* in Argentina, Chile, Uruguay and Paraguay and *churrasco* (*shoo-ras-koo*) in Brazil. Both of these terms are now commonly used to describe not only a way of cooking, but a broader social event — the two cannot be separated. The events have evolved to become favourite national pastimes. In the countries of South America, no celebration, gathering or weekend is complete without a barbecue!

There are some unique differences between these two traditional cooking styles. The *asados* take whole splayed carcasses or large sections of meat and thread them onto metal crosses, which are then fixed into the ground around the hot coals of a wood fire. The meat is grilled slowly, imparting a smoky flavour to the meat. Smaller pieces of meat, or sausages and sweetmeats are often cooked on metal grill plates, known as *parrillas*, which are set over hot coals. Outdoor wood fire ovens, known as *hornos*, can also be used to roast large pieces of meat.

In Brazil, a *churrasco* barbecue involves the meat (the traditional cut known as *picanha*), chicken or sausage being threaded onto long metal skewers, or barbecue swords, and fixed onto a rotisserie where they are cooked over hot coals. Once cooked, the meat is sliced directly from the barbecue swords onto guests' plates and served with piquant salsas and sauces, salads and complementary side dishes. Recipes for chicken, fish and seafood are sometimes marinated in herb and spice mixes or rolled and stuffed, and can be teamed with a selection of simpler sides.

For the modern home cook, recipes in this book have been written to suit the more convenient gas-style home barbecues. If you have the space, time and patience, then grilling over hot coal or wood-style barbecues will improve the meat's lovely smoky flavour and contribute to the authenticity of the occasion. Rotisserie attachments are readily available and can easily be fitted to most barbecues that have a lid.

South American grilling is as much about entertaining as it is about taste and flavour. The focus is on bringing family and friends together — it is not uncommon for the grill to be fired up all afternoon with drinks being passed around and various dishes being offered at different times and shared throughout the day. You can get ideas for dishes by consulting the structured menu plans that have been designed to suit Lazy Summer Afternoons (pages 26–27), Friday Nights with your Mates (pages 68–69), Family Gatherings (pages 116–117) or a traditional Brazilian Churrasco Feast (pages 158–159).

Or, simply choose a couple of your favourite grills and team them with a selection of side dishes and salads. Of course, no South American meal would be complete without one or two sauces and salsas — bursting with flavour, they are a must alongside most grilled meats.

A variety of appetisers have been included in the first chapter — these are perfect for grazing on while the main grills are cooking and the perfect way to kick-start any gathering. Similarly, a range of traditional colourful cocktails (pages 188–203) are easy and quick to make, but best of all they'll keep your guests feeling refreshed. And, what better way to finish off a wonderful meal than with a super-sweet caramel-inspired dessert partnered with meringue or a soft biscuity pastry, or keep it simple with grilled caramelised fruit and sorbet (pages 164–187).

Most of the recipes in this book are pleasingly simple, while the more complex ones can be prepared in advance, which helps to keep you relaxed and free to socialise and enjoy the occasion. So, what are you waiting for? Pour yourself a drink and throw yourself into an all-day South American grilling feast!

APPETISERS AND STARTERS

CANCHA

TOASTED CORN SNACK

These traditional snacks from Peru are great served with a beer and make the perfect start to a barbecue. The key ingredient, *maiz mote pelado*, are large dried white corn kernels and are available at Latin American food stores or can be purchased online. These corn kernels make a soft popping sound as they expand but do not fluff out in the same way as popcorn does, instead becoming deliciously crisp and crunchy.

2 CUPS (320 G/11 OZ) MAIZ MOTE PELADO
    (GIANT WHITE CORN)
2 TABLESPOONS VEGETABLE OIL
2 TEASPOONS SEA SALT
1 TEASPOON SMOKED PAPRIKA

Soak the *maiz mote pelado* in a bowl of cold water for 12 hours. Drain and spread out on a clean tea towel for 1 hour, to dry.

Heat the oil in a large heavy-based saucepan over medium heat. When the oil is hot but not smoking, add the corn and toss to coat in the oil. Cover and cook, shaking occasionally, for 10 minutes, or until the kernels are golden brown. Drain on paper towels and allow to cool.

When you are ready to serve, transfer the corn to a large bowl, sprinkle with the salt and paprika and toss to coat.

SERVES 8

BROCHETA DE RIÑÓN A LA PARRILLA

GRILLED KIDNEY SKEWERS

Offal is commonly served at a South American *asado*. The kidneys are soaked prior to cooking to help reduce their strong aroma and taste. They cook beautifully on the barbecue — grill them until they are just pink in the centre. Avoid over-cooking, as this will cause them to become tough.

8 BAMBOO SKEWERS

6 LAMB KIDNEYS

1 TABLESPOON SEA SALT

2 TEASPOONS WHITE VINEGAR

40 G (1½ OZ) BUTTER, MELTED

LEMON WEDGES, TO SERVE

Soak the bamboo skewers in cold water for 30 minutes to prevent them from burning during cooking. Rinse the kidneys under cold running water.

Fill a medium-sized bowl with cold water. Add the salt and vinegar and stir to dissolve the salt. Place the kidneys in the water, cover, and refrigerate for 1 hour.

Drain the kidneys and pat dry with paper towels. Slice each kidney lengthwise into four thin slices and thread onto the skewers.

Preheat a barbecue chargrill to medium–high. Brush the kidneys with a little of the melted butter and season with freshly ground black pepper. Cook the skewers for 2 minutes on each side, or until just cooked — they should still be a little pink inside. Squeeze with lemon juice, and serve immediately.

MAKES 8

PERUVIAN CEVICHE

Peruvian ceviche differs from other variations of this dish, as it is only marinated or 'cooked' in citrus juice for a short period of time, about 30 minutes. You can even drink the 'juice', known as *leche de tigre*, afterwards if you so desire. You will need to use about 20 limes for this dish.

I KG (2 LB 3 OZ) SKINLESS AND BONELESS
   KINGFISH, ROCKLING OR OTHER
   DELICATELY FLAVOURED FISH FILLETS

2 CUPS (500 ML/17 FL OZ) LIME JUICE

2 GARLIC CLOVES, FINELY CHOPPED

2 LONG RED CHILLIES, SEEDED AND FINELY
   CHOPPED

I TEASPOON SEA SALT

2 SWEET POTATOES, PEELED AND CUT INTO
   1.5 CM (½ INCH) THICK ROUNDS

I RED ONION, THINLY SLICED

½ CUP CANCHA (PAGE 12), WITHOUT
   THE SEASONING

I LARGE HANDFUL CORIANDER (CILANTRO)
   LEAVES, CHOPPED

OLIVE OIL, FOR DRIZZLING

Slice the fish thinly across the grain and then into 2.5 cm (1 inch) wide pieces. Place in a non-reactive bowl. Add the lime juice, garlic, chilli and salt and stir to combine. Gently push the fish down so it is submerged in the lime juice. Cover and refrigerate for 30 minutes.

Meanwhile, cook the sweet potato in a saucepan of boiling water for 8–10 minutes, or until just tender. Drain and set aside to cool.

Soak the onion in cold water for 10 minutes — this will help to mellow the flavour — then drain well and stir through the fish mixture to combine.

Transfer the fish and its marinating liquid to a serving bowl and sprinkle the *cancha* and coriander over the top. Season the sweet potato and drizzle with olive oil just before serving.

SERVES 10–12

PERUVIAN CEVICHE

PROVOLETA

GRILLED PROVOLONE WITH OREGANO AND CHILLI

Grilling provolone cheese is very common in both Argentina and Brazil. It is easy to prepare at the start of a meal and is eaten straight from the hotplate early in the proceedings, while the larger cuts of meat are slow-cooking.

500 G (I LB 2 OZ) PROVOLONE CHEESE, CUT INTO 1.5 CM (½ INCH) THICK SLICES

2 TEASPOONS SEA SALT

2 TEASPOONS DRIED OREGANO

I TEASPOON DRIED CHILLI FLAKES

OLIVE OIL, FOR BRUSHING

Preheat a barbecue chargrill or hotplate to medium–high.

Arrange the provolone on a tray. Combine the salt, oregano and chilli flakes in a small bowl and sprinkle over both sides of the provolone, pressing lightly into the cheese to adhere the flavourings.

Brush a little olive oil over the chargrill (or you can use a cast-iron frying pan) and cook the provolone for 2 minutes on each side, or until it is golden brown but still holding its shape. Transfer the cheese slices to a serving plate and serve immediately.

SERVES 8

PÃO DE ALHO GRELHADO

GRILLED BRAZILIAN GARLIC BREAD

Unlike the garlic bread we are accustomed to in the West, this Brazilian-style version is topped with thick onion, garlic and mayonnaise. It is only grilled on one side, just enough to crisp the base, while the sauce is lightly heated through and becomes full of flavour.

1 ONION, FINELY CHOPPED

2 GARLIC CLOVES, FINELY CHOPPED

1½ CUPS (355 G/12 OZ) GOOD-QUALITY
   WHOLE-EGG MAYONNAISE

80 G (3 OZ) BUTTER, AT ROOM TEMPERATURE

2 CRUSTY BAGUETTES

Preheat a barbecue chargrill to medium.

Combine the onion, garlic, mayonnaise and butter in a bowl, season with sea salt and mix well to combine.

Cut the baguettes into quarters and then in half lengthwise down the middle. Spread the mayonnaise mixture generously over the cut sides of each quarter.

Grill the bread, crust side down, for 3–4 minutes, or until the butter has melted and the bread is heated through and golden brown. Serve hot.

SERVES 8–16

MUSSARELA GRELHADA

GRILLED MOZZARELLA WITH CHEIRO VERDE SAUCE

Cheiro verde, or 'smells green', is the Brazilian term for the combination of spring onions, parsley and coriander that are often sold tied together in bunches. The herbs are traditionally cut fresh and served with fish, but here they have been combined with olive oil, chilli and garlic and turned into a delicious sauce.

OLIVE OIL, FOR BRUSHING

500 G (1 LB 2 OZ) MOZZARELLA CHEESE, CUT INTO 1.5 CM (½ INCH) THICK SLICES

½ TEASPOON SEA SALT (OPTIONAL)

CHEIRO VERDE SAUCE

1 LONG RED CHILLI, SEEDED AND FINELY CHOPPED

1 GARLIC CLOVE, FINELY CHOPPED

½ TEASPOON SEA SALT

6 SPRING ONIONS (SCALLIONS), FINELY CHOPPED

1 LARGE HANDFUL FLAT-LEAF (ITALIAN) PARSLEY, FINELY CHOPPED

1 LARGE HANDFUL CORIANDER (CILANTRO) LEAVES, FINELY CHOPPED

2 TABLESPOONS OLIVE OIL

To make the *cheiro verde* sauce, put the chilli, garlic and salt in a large mortar and use a pestle to pound to a paste. Transfer to a small bowl, add the spring onion, parsley and coriander and stir to combine. Mix in the olive oil, then transfer to a small serving dish.

Preheat a barbecue chargrill or hotplate to medium–high. Brush a little olive oil over the chargrill and arrange the mozzarella slices on top, seasoning with sea salt, if using. Grill the mozzarella for 2 minutes on each side, or until it is golden brown but still holding its shape.

Transfer the cheese slices to a serving plate and serve hot with the *cheiro verde* sauce drizzled over the top.

SERVES 8

CORAÇÃO DE FRANGO GRELHADO

GRILLED CHICKEN HEARTS

A popular starter to a Brazilian grill, these chicken hearts are first marinated in fresh herbs before being threaded onto skewers and quickly cooked on the barbecue. They make a great alternative to other meats, and although relatively high in cholesterol, are a good source of protein and B vitamins. Although common in Brazil, they can be difficult to source elsewhere — ask your butcher to order them for you in advance.

1 KG (2 LB 3 OZ) CHICKEN HEARTS

½ LARGE BROWN ONION, THINLY SLICED

JUICE OF 2 LEMONS

2 TABLESPOONS FINELY CHOPPED OREGANO LEAVES

2 TABLESPOONS FINELY CHOPPED FLAT-LEAF (ITALIAN) PARSLEY, PLUS EXTRA TO SERVE

1 GARLIC CLOVE, FINELY CHOPPED

3 LONG METAL BARBECUE SKEWERS

VEGETABLE OIL, FOR BRUSHING

LEMON WEDGES, TO SERVE

Trim and discard the membrane from the chicken hearts and remove any excess fat.

Combine the onion, lemon juice, oregano, parsley and garlic in a non-reactive bowl. Add the chicken hearts, season with sea salt and freshly ground black pepper and turn to coat the chicken. Cover and leave to marinate in the refrigerator for 2–4 hours.

Remove the chicken hearts from the marinade and thread them onto the metal skewers — you should get about ten on each skewer.

Preheat a barbecue chargrill to medium–high. Brush a little vegetable oil over the chargrill and cook the chicken heart skewers for 10 minutes, turning frequently, until golden brown and just cooked through.

You can use a fork to push the chicken hearts off the skewers or simply serve them sprinkled with extra parsley and lemon wedges on the side for guests to help themselves.

SERVES 12

LAZY SUMMER AFTERNOONS

SERVES 10–12

1½ × PORTIONS CANCHA (TOASTED CORN SNACK) 12
PERUVIAN CEVICHE 15
WHOLE ROASTED SIRLOIN WITH CHIMICHURRI 42
ARGENTINIAN GRILLED GARLIC AND ROSEMARY FLAT BREAD 155
2 × PORTIONS LIMA BEAN SALAD 144
2 × PORTIONS GRILLED RED CAPSICUM 138
PERUVIAN CARAMEL AND MERINGUE PIE 180
BATIDA DE MANGO 190

THE NIGHT BEFORE:

- Soak the *maiz mote pelado* for the Cancha

MORNING OF:

- Drain and prepare the Cancha, setting ½ cup aside (unseasoned) for Ceviche
- Prepare *Chimichurri*
- Prepare Lima Bean Salad
- Prepare base for Caramel and Meringue Pie, refrigerate

2 HOURS BEFORE GUESTS ARRIVE:

- Marinate sirloin in *Chimichurri*
- Prepare Grilled Red Capsicum

1 HOUR BEFORE GUESTS ARRIVE:

- Prepare dough for Argentinian Grilled Garlic and Rosemary Flat Bread and set aside to prove
- Prepare ingredients for Ceviche, cover separately and refrigerate — do not combine
- Set up bar for making Batidas

UPON GUESTS' ARRIVAL:

- Make a large jug of Mango Batida and serve
- Serve Cancha
- Combine Ceviche ingredients and refrigerate for 30 minutes
- Preheat the barbecue
- Put the sirloin on the barbecue to cook
- Serve Ceviche
- Knock back the bread dough, roll into balls, cover and set aside to prove
- Check sirloin, remove, cover and rest, once cooked
- Grill Flat Bread
- Slice sirloin and serve with Lima Bean Salad, Grilled Capsicum and Flat Bread
- Finish preparing Caramel and Meringue Pie — refrigerate until chilled or ready to serve
- Serve Caramel and Meringue Pie when ready

EMPANADAS MENDOCINAS

BAKED ARGENTINIAN SPICED BEEF EMPANADAS

Empanadas are a popular snack throughout South America. They can be found baked or deep-fried and stuffed with a variety of sweet or savoury fillings. This version of these little hand-held pies originates from the Mendoza province in the mid-west of Argentina, bordering Chile. They are filled with spiced meat, egg and olives and are then baked in the oven or on the barbecue.

FILLING

60 G (2 OZ) BUTTER

1 LARGE ONION, FINELY CHOPPED

2 GARLIC CLOVES, FINELY CHOPPED

1 TEASPOON GROUND CUMIN

1 TEASPOON SMOKED HOT PAPRIKA

1 TEASPOON DRIED CHILLI FLAKES

¼ CUP (60 ML/2 FL OZ) OLIVE OIL, PLUS
    EXTRA FOR GREASING

400 G (14 OZ) BEEF SIRLOIN, TRIMMED
    AND FINELY DICED

2 LARGE HARD-BOILED EGGS, PEELED
    AND ROUGHLY CHOPPED

½ CUP (90 G/3¼ OZ) PITTED GREEN
    OLIVES, ROUGHLY CHOPPED

3 SPRING ONIONS (SCALLIONS), GREEN
    PART ONLY, SLICED

2 TABLESPOONS FINELY CHOPPED
    OREGANO LEAVES

CHIMICHURRI (PAGE 108), TO SERVE

PASTRY

80 G (3 OZ) BUTTER, CUBED

2 TEASPOONS SALT

3 CUPS (450 G/1 LB) PLAIN (ALL-PURPOSE)
    FLOUR, PLUS EXTRA FOR DUSTING

1 LARGE EGG, LIGHTLY BEATEN, PLUS
    EXTRA FOR BRUSHING

To make the filling, melt the butter in a large frying pan over low–medium heat. Cook the onion and garlic until softened. Add the cumin, paprika and chilli flakes and cook until fragrant. Transfer to a bowl and set aside. Return the pan to the heat, add the olive oil and increase the heat to high. Cook the beef, in batches, for 3–4 minutes each, or until browned all over. Remove from the heat.

Combine the beef with the onion mixture in a medium-sized bowl and set aside for 15 minutes to cool slightly. Add the egg, olives, spring onion and oregano and stir to combine. Season with sea salt and freshly ground black pepper. Cover and refrigerate for 30 minutes, or until cooled.

Meanwhile, to make the pastry, put ¾ cup (185 ml/6½ fl oz) water in a small saucepan over low–medium heat. Add the butter and salt and heat until the butter melts and the salt has dissolved. Remove from the heat.

Place the flour in a medium-sized bowl, add the water mixture and the egg and stir to form a rough dough. Turn out onto a lightly floured work surface and knead for 2–3 minutes to form a smooth elastic dough. Shape into a disc, wrap in plastic wrap and refrigerate for 30 minutes.

Preheat the oven to 200°C (400°F), or use a gas barbecue fitted with a lid. Lightly grease two baking trays with olive oil.

To assemble the empanadas, cut the dough in half (keep one half in plastic wrap to prevent it from drying out). Roll out the remaining dough on a lightly floured work surface to 3 mm (¼ inch) thick all over. Using a 10 cm (4 inch) round pastry cutter, cut about 30 round circles.

Divide half of the filling evenly among the circles, placing tablespoonfuls in the centre of each. Lightly moisten the pastry edges with water and fold in half to enclose the filling and form a half-moon shape. Pinch along the edge to seal and enclose the filling. Arrange the empanadas on the prepared baking trays and brush the tops with the lightly beaten egg. Repeat with the remaining dough and filling until all the mixture is used.

Cook the empanadas in the oven for 15–20 minutes, or until golden brown. If you are using a gas barbecue, turn off the middle burners and place the trays on top to cook. Serve the empanadas hot with the *chimichurri* on the side.

MAKES 30

BAKED ARGENTINIAN SPICED BEEF EMPANADAS

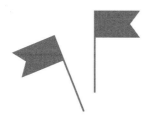

AREPAS DE QUESO

GRILLED CORNBREAD STUFFED WITH CHEESE

Arepas are a common snack food or starter served at Venezuelan restaurants or street stalls, known as *areperias*. They are small round fried cornbreads, which can be stuffed with a variety of fillings, from simple cheeses to slow-cooked meats.

2 CUPS (360 G/12½ OZ) MASAREPA (SEE NOTE)

2 TEASPOONS VEGETABLE OIL

1 TEASPOON SEA SALT

BUTTER, FOR BRUSHING

1½ CUPS (190 G/6½ OZ) GRATED QUESO
    FRESCO OR MOZZARELLA CHEESE

GUASACACA (PAGE 114), TO SERVE

Place the masarepa in a medium-sized bowl. Add the oil, salt and 1½ cups (375 ml/12½ fl oz) water and stir to combine. Turn out onto a clean work surface and knead to form a smooth dough, adding a little more water if the dough is too dry.

Divide the dough into twelve even-sized portions and shape each portion into a ball. Flatten each ball to make a disc, about 1 cm (½ inch) thick all over.

Preheat a barbecue chargrill or hotplate to medium. Brush a little butter over the chargrill plate and cook the *arepas*, in batches, for 2 minutes on each side, or until golden.

When all of the *arepas* are cooked, cut them in half crosswise, being careful not to cut all the way through. Stuff with cheese and grill for a further 20 seconds on each side, or until the cheese has melted. Serve hot with the *Guasacaca* on the side or spread over the cheese.

NOTE: *Masarepa is a pre-cooked corn flour and is available from Latin American food stores.*

MAKES 12

ESPETINHO GRELHADO DE QUEIJO COALHO
GRILLED HALOUMI SKEWERS

The cheese used for this dish in Brazil is known as *queijo de coalho* — a dense salty, white-yellow cheese that is difficult to source outside its country of origin, so haloumi is the next best substitute. These skewers are drizzled with molasses, but you can serve them much like saganaki, with a squeeze of lemon, if you wish.

8 BAMBOO SKEWERS

185 G (6½ OZ) HALOUMI, CUT INTO 2 CM (¾ INCH) THICK SLICES, THEN IN HALF LENGTHWISE

OLIVE OIL, FOR BRUSHING

1 TABLESPOON MOLASSES

Soak the bamboo skewers in cold water for 30 minutes to prevent them from burning during cooking.

Thread the haloumi pieces evenly onto the bamboo skewers.

Preheat a barbecue chargrill or hotplate to medium–high.
Brush a little olive oil over the chargrill and cook the haloumi for 4–5 minutes, turning occasionally, until golden brown on both sides. Serve immediately, with the molasses drizzled over the top.

SERVES 4–8

ESPETINHO DE DRUMET DE FRANGO GRELHADO

GRILLED CHICKEN DRUMMETTE SKEWERS

Chicken drummettes are part of the wing joint, where the end of the wing is cut off, leaving the base, which looks much like a drumstick. When chargrilled they are packed with flavour and very moreish.

1 KG (2 LB 3 OZ) CHICKEN DRUMMETTES

ROCK SALT, FOR SEASONING

8 LONG METAL BARBECUE SKEWERS

VEGETABLE OIL, FOR BRUSHING

Preheat a barbecue chargrill or hotplate to medium.

To thread the drummettes onto the skewers, pierce a skewer through the fat just underneath the bone at the 'stick end' of the drummette. Continue until there are five drummettes on the skewer, making sure there is a slight gap between each one to help them cook evenly. Take a second skewer and pierce through the flesh underneath the bone at the opposite end of the drummettes — alternating the drummettes between skewers in this way will ensure even cooking. Repeat with the remaining drummettes and skewers. Season the chicken skewers with rock salt.

Brush a little vegetable oil over the chargrill and cook the chicken skewers for 20–25 minutes, turning frequently, until they are cooked through, crispy and golden brown. Brush off any excess salt.

To serve, use a barbecue fork to push the drummettes off the skewers for guests to help themselves.

NOTE: Drummettes can be threaded onto skewers in advance and stored in the refrigerator. Bring back to room temperature before grilling. Do not season with rock salt until just before you are ready to grill as the chicken will absorb the salt and the flesh will become too salty.

SERVES 8–10

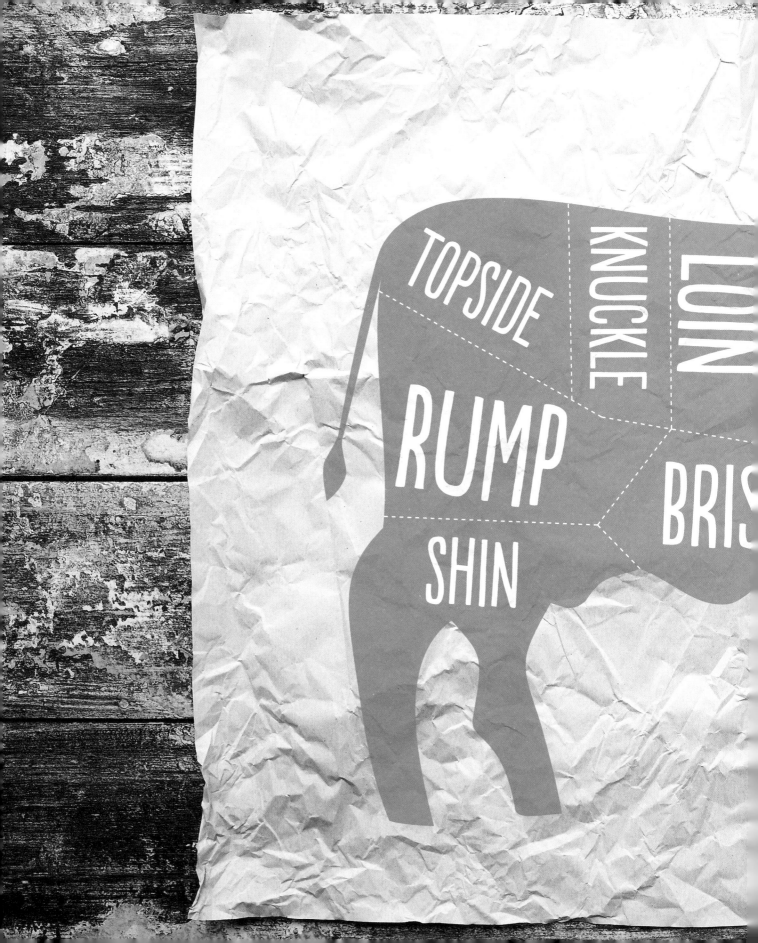

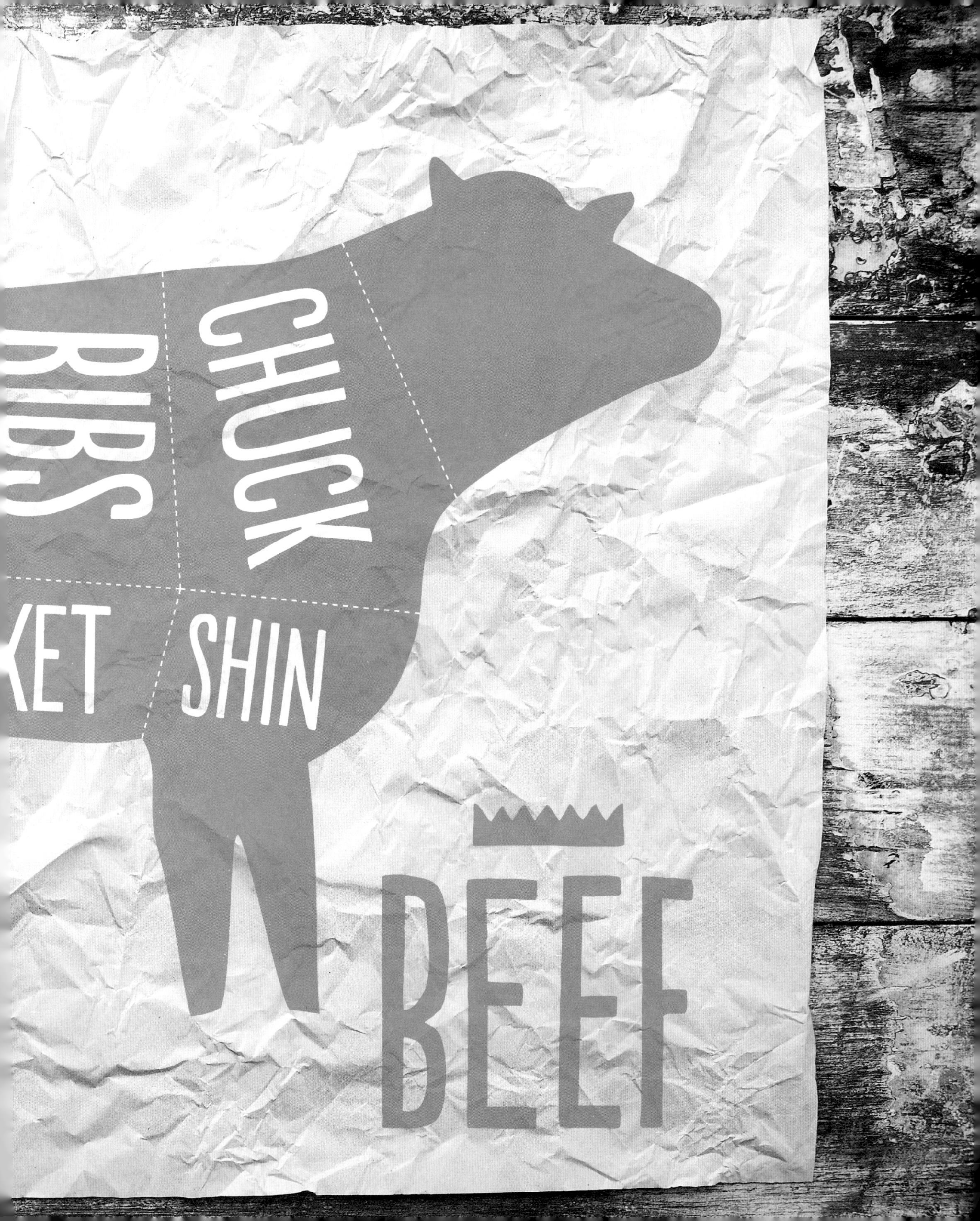
RIBS
CHUCK
KET
SHIN
BEEF

ANTICUCHOS DE CORAZÓN

OX HEART KEBABS

These kebabs are marinated in a paste that includes *aji panca*, or Peruvian dark red chillies. They have a mild heat and fruity flavour and are made into a paste that can often be found in Latin American food stores or online. If you can source dried *panca* chillies, you can seed them and soak them in boiling water for 30 minutes to soften, before draining and blending to a smooth paste. If neither is available, you can substitute with any other mild red chilli paste.

12 BAMBOO SKEWERS

1 OX HEART (ABOUT 800 G/1 LB 12 OZ)

½ CUP (125 ML/4 FL OZ) RED WINE VINEGAR

2 TABLESPOONS VEGETABLE OIL, PLUS EXTRA
FOR BRUSHING

2 TABLESPOONS AJI PANCA PASTE

6 GARLIC CLOVES, CRUSHED

1 TABLESPOON GROUND CUMIN

2 TEASPOONS SEA SALT

Soak the bamboo skewers in cold water for 30 minutes to prevent them from burning during cooking.

Clean the ox heart, removing the skin, sinew and any excess fat. Cut into 1.5 cm (½ inch) thick slices and then into 2.5 cm (1 inch) bite-sized pieces.

Combine the remaining ingredients in a non-reactive bowl. Add the ox heart and toss to coat. Cover and leave to marinate in the refrigerator for at least 4 hours or overnight.

Reserving the marinade, remove the ox heart and thread the pieces onto the pre-soaked skewers.

Preheat a barbecue chargrill to medium–high. Brush a little vegetable oil over the chargrill and cook the skewers for 3 minutes on each side, basting with the reserved marinade as they cook, until the kebabs are just cooked through.

VARIATION: You can substitute thinly sliced rump steak or chicken breast for ox heart, if desired. If they are sliced thinly, the cooking times will be the same.

SERVES 12

MAINS

SOLOMILLO ASADO CON CHIMICHURRI

WHOLE ROASTED SIRLOIN
WITH CHIMICHURRI

This dish is ideal for large gatherings. Marinated in the traditional Argentinian *asado* accompaniment, *chimichurri* (green sauce), it is succulent and full-flavoured. Simply slice and serve with additional *chimichurri* for extra zing and colour.

2.5 KG (5½ LB) WHOLE BEEF SIRLOIN

2 PORTIONS CHIMICHURRI (PAGE 108)

Trim the sirloin of any excess fat and sinew, leaving a layer about 5 mm (¼ inch) thick. Score the fat using a large sharp knife. Place the sirloin on a wire rack and set in a large roasting tray. Rub half of the *Chimichurri* over the fat. Cover and leave to marinate in the refrigerator for 2–4 hours.

Preheat a gas barbecue with a lid to 180°C (350°F). All the burners should be set to medium. (You can also use a charcoal barbecue but you will need to make sure the coals can maintain the heat.)

Insert a meat thermometer into the centre of the meat. Fill the tray with 1 cm (½ inch) water underneath the meat. Place the tray in the centre of the barbecue and turn off the burners directly underneath. Close the lid and cook for 1–1¼ hours for medium, or until the meat thermometer reads 55°C (131°F).

Remove the tray from the barbecue, cover with foil and set aside to rest for 15 minutes. Cut the sirloin into slices and serve with the remaining *Chimichurri*. It also goes well served with Grilled Red Capsicum (page 138), Salt-baked Potatoes (page 128) and Argentinian Grilled Garlic and Rosemary Flat Bread (page 155).

SERVES 10

PICANHA

RUMP CAP

Picanha is considered the best cut of beef in Brazil. It is the rump cap, which has a thick layer of fat covering the meat — this slowly melts (or renders down) when cooked slowly over indirect heat, adding flavour to the meat and keeping it moist and tender. Traditionally, the rump cap is sliced into thick steaks, threaded onto sword-like skewers and cooked on a rotisserie. If you can't find the right kind of skewers (these can be purchased online) you can cook the steaks individually on a barbecue chargrill.

Picanha is not a common cut, so you'll need to ask your butcher to specially cut the rump cap for you. You may still have to buy the other parts of the rump too, but these can be frozen and used another day.

1 KG (2 LB 3 OZ) WHOLE PICANHA
   (RUMP CAP)
1 LARGE BRAZILIAN-STYLE METAL
   SKEWER (CHURRASCO SWORD)
ROCK SALT, FOR SEASONING

VEGETABLE OIL, FOR GREASING
FAROFA (PAGE 120), TO SERVE
VINAGRETE (PAGE 115), TO SERVE

Preheat a barbecue chargrill to medium–high. Alternatively, preheat a gas barbecue fitted with a rotisserie to 200°C (400°F) and set the burners to medium, keeping the lid closed.

Using a sharp knife, slice the *picanha* into 4 cm (1½ inch) thick steaks. You should get approximately four steaks.

To thread the steaks onto the churrasco sword or rotisserie attachment (if using), insert the skewer through the fat at one end of the steak and back up through the fat at the other end, curving the fat to form a 'C' shape. Continue threading the remaining steaks onto the same skewer or rod. Season the meat generously with rock salt on both sides.

If using a rotisserie, secure the spit according to the manufacturer's instructions. Turn off the two middle burners and place a drip tray filled with 1 cm (½ inch) water underneath the meat. Cook for 15–20 minutes for medium, or until cooked to your liking. Wearing barbecue mitts, carefully remove the rotisserie rod.

Alternatively, lightly brush the chargrill plate with vegetable oil. Grill the meat for 6–8 minutes on each side for medium–rare, or until cooked to your liking.

To serve, brush off any excess salt and use a sharp knife to thinly slice the meat directly onto serving plates, allowing the juices to be caught underneath. Return the *picanha* to the chargrill to re-sear the outside if desired. Serve with *farofa* and *vinagrete* on the side.

NOTE: Picanha can be threaded in advance and refrigerated. Bring back to room temperature before grilling. Do not season with rock salt until you are ready to grill.

SERVES 4–6

PICANHA WITH FAROFA AND VINAGRETE

PIERNA DE CORDERO A LA SAL

SALT-BAKED LAMB SHOULDER STUFFED WITH ANCHOVY, ROSEMARY AND GARLIC

This dish is unique in that the salt forms a crust around the meat, sealing in all of the natural juices and locking in the moisture, while at the same time imparting a surprisingly subtle salty flavour to the lamb — when the salt crust is cracked it releases a mouth-watering aroma.

1 SMALL HANDFUL ROSEMARY LEAVES

4 GARLIC CLOVES, CRUSHED

10 ANCHOVY FILLETS

FINELY GRATED ZEST OF 1 LEMON

2 TABLESPOONS LEMON JUICE

1 TABLESPOON OLIVE OIL

2 KG (4 LB 6 OZ) LAMB SHOULDER, BONED
  AND BUTTERFLIED

4 KG (8 LB 12 OZ) TABLE SALT

Combine the rosemary, garlic, anchovies and lemon zest in a small food processor and process until finely chopped. Add the lemon juice and olive oil and process to make a smooth paste.

Preheat a gas barbecue with a lid to 200°C (400°F). All the burners should be set to medium.

Lay the lamb out, skin side down, on a clean work surface. Season with sea salt and freshly ground black pepper, then rub over the anchovy paste to coat one side. Roll the lamb shoulder up tightly, tucking in any loose ends. Tie with kitchen string to secure.

Pour the table salt into a clean kitchen sink, add 1½ cups (375 ml/12½ fl oz) water and mix with your hands to moisten and make the salt compact, adding a little more water if required.

Put half of the salt in the base of a large roasting tray. Place the rolled shoulder on top and cover with the remaining salt, pressing to create a salt crust, about 1 cm (½ inch) thick all over. Pack the salt around the lamb, to completely cover.

Place the tray in the centre of the barbecue and turn off the burners directly underneath. Cover and cook the lamb for 3 hours.

Remove the tray from the barbecue and set aside to rest the meat for 15 minutes. To serve, crack the salt using the end of a rolling pin. Break away the salt to expose the lamb. Remove the lamb, dusting off any excess salt, then place on a chopping board and cut into slices to serve. This dish goes well with Brazilian Rice (page 122), Grilled Red Capsicum (page 138) and Lentil Stew (page 134).

SERVES 6–8

CHIVITO

GRILLED BEEF SANDWICH

Chivito is considered Uruguay's national dish, it translates as 'baby goat' in Spanish, although it is made using beef. It is not for the faint-hearted or those with high cholesterol, with multiple layers of meat, egg and cheese! This recipe serves one, but if you want more, simply increase the amount of ingredients accordingly.

125 G (4 OZ) BEEF FILLET, SLICED ABOUT
    5 MM (¼ INCH) THICK

VEGETABLE OIL, FOR DRIZZLING

2 SLICES SHORT-CUT BACON

1 EGG

BUTTER, FOR SPREADING

1 LARGE CRUSTY SANDWICH ROLL,
    CUT INTO HALVES

2–3 TABLESPOONS GOOD-QUALITY
    WHOLE-EGG MAYONNAISE

2 SLICES HAM

2 SLICES MOZZARELLA CHEESE

TOMATO SLICES

4 GREEN PITTED OLIVES, SLICED

LETTUCE LEAVES

Preheat a barbecue hotplate to medium–high. Preheat an overhead griller (broiler) to high heat (this is to melt the cheese and finish off the sandwich once the meat is cooked).

Drizzle the beef with a little vegetable oil and season with sea salt and freshly ground black pepper. Cook the beef and bacon for 1–2 minutes on each side, or until crisp and golden brown. Remove from the heat and keep warm.

Meanwhile, crack the egg onto the hotplate and cook to your liking, then remove from the heat and keep warm.

To assemble the sandwich, butter the roll and spread with mayonnaise. Place the steak on the base of the roll, top with the bacon, ham and cheese and set under the griller, until the cheese has melted. Place the tomato, egg, olives and lastly the lettuce on top. Cover with the other half of the sandwich roll and serve hot.

MAKES 1

SALMON HORNEADO A LA SAL CON MANTECA, HIERBAS Y LIMÓN

SALT-BAKED SALMON STUFFED WITH HERBS, BUTTER AND LEMON

When moistened, salt clumps and compacts together, allowing it to be moulded around the fish to create a clay-oven effect. The fish is completely encased in the salt preventing the cooking juices from evaporating, and keeping the fish moist and succulent while enhancing its natural flavour. This dish goes especially well with *Salsa Criolla* or *Pebre*.

2.5 KG (5½ LB) WHOLE SALMON,
   CLEANED AND SCALED
I LEMON, SLICED INTO ROUNDS
12 SPRIGS THYME
2 SPRIGS SAGE

2 SPRIGS OREGANO
40 G (1½ OZ) BUTTER, THINLY SLICED
4 KG (8 LB 12 OZ) TABLE SALT
SALSA CRIOLLA (PAGE 110) OR PEBRE
   (PAGE 111), TO SERVE

Rinse the salmon under cold running water and pat dry with paper towels. Season the cavity of the fish with sea salt and freshly ground black pepper. Stuff with the lemon slices, fresh herbs and butter.

Preheat a gas barbecue with a lid to 200°C (400°F). All the burners should be set to medium. Pour the salt into a clean kitchen sink, add 1½ cups (375 ml/12½ fl oz) water and mix with your hands to moisten and make the salt compact, adding a little more water if required.

Transfer half of the salt into a roasting tray large enough to fit the fish — cut off the head and trim the tail, if necessary. Place the stuffed salmon on top and cover with the remaining salt, to create a salt crust about 1 cm (½ inch) thick. Pack the salt around the fish, to completely cover.

Place the tray in the centre of the barbecue and turn off the burners directly underneath. Close the lid and cook for 1 hour. Remove the tray from the barbecue and set aside to rest for 15 minutes.

Crack the salt using the end of a rolling pin and break away the crust to expose the salmon. Remove and discard the salmon skin. Use a spatula to serve portions of the top fillet, then peel away the backbone to serve the remaining fillet. Serve with *Salsa Criolla* or *Pebre*.

SERVES 10–12

SALT-BAKED SALMON STUFFED WITH HERBS, BUTTER AND LEMON

TIRA DE ASADO

ASADO RIB STRIPS

A unique Argentinian cut, these ribs are cross-cut through the bone to create long narrow rib strips, known as *asado* — ask your butcher to do this for you. This style of cut shortens the tough fibres of the meat allowing them to be grilled on the barbecue relatively quickly. They are seasoned with rock salt to bring out the flavour of the meat without making it excessively salty. Substitute short ribs, if unavailable. *Asado* is traditionally cooked over hot coals — you can create these by burning wood or charcoal until it becomes white. Spread the coals out evenly and top with a grill rack set about 15 cm (6 inches) above the coals. Grilling the ribs over wood coals will impart a delicious smoky flavour to the meat.

2 KG (4 LB 6 OZ) ASADO CUT SHORT BEEF
   RIB STRIPS
ROCK SALT
VEGETABLE OIL, FOR BRUSHING
CHIMICHURRI (PAGE 108), TO SERVE
SALT-BAKED POTATOES (PAGE 128), TO SERVE

Preheat a barbecue chargrill to medium.

Season the ribs generously with rock salt. Brush a little vegetable oil over the chargrill and cook the ribs for 10–15 minutes on each side for medium–rare, or until lightly charred on the outside and cooked to your liking.

Brush off any excess salt. Remove from the heat, cover and set aside to rest for 10 minutes before serving. Transfer to a chopping board and use a large sharp knife to slice.

Serve the rib strips with *Chimichurri* and Salt-baked Potatoes.

SERVES 6

MEDALLONES ENVUELTOS EN PANCETTA

BACON-WRAPPED FILLET MIGNON

The bacon adds a lovely smoky flavour to the meat as well as adding extra fat, to help keep this trim cut moist. Requiring only brief cooking time, this dish makes for sophisticated barbecue fare when served with Potatoes with Spicy Yellow Cheese Sauce (pages 160–161) .

4 SLICES RINDLESS SHORT-CUT BACON

4 x I50 G (5 OZ) BEEF TENDERLOIN STEAKS
    (FILLET MIGNON)

ROCK SALT, FOR SEASONING

VEGETABLE OIL, FOR BRUSHING

Wrap a slice of bacon around the circumference of each of the steaks. Tie with kitchen string to secure and help the steaks hold their shape; season with rock salt and freshly ground black pepper.

Preheat a barbecue chargrill or hotplate to high. Brush a little vegetable oil over the chargrill and cook the steaks, bacon side down, for 5 minutes, until lightly charred all over. Turn the meat and cook the other side for 3 minutes for medium–rare, or until cooked to your liking.

Brush off any excess salt, transfer the steaks to a tray, cover with foil and leave to rest for 5 minutes. Remove the kitchen string and serve hot with Potatoes with Spicy Yellow Cheese Sauce.

SERVES 4

COSTILLA DE CORDERO EN COSTRA DE ACEITUNAS

LAMB RACK WITH OLIVE CRUST

The flavours in this delicious lamb rack reflect the strong influence Italian cooking has had on Argentinian cuisine. This dish looks beautiful and will be a well-received addition to any barbecue gathering.

OLIVE CRUST

1 CUP (150 G/5 OZ) PITTED KALAMATA OLIVES

2 GARLIC CLOVES, CHOPPED

1 TABLESPOON CAPERS, RINSED AND
    SQUEEZED DRY

2 ANCHOVY FILLETS

FINELY GRATED ZEST OF 1 LEMON

1½ CUPS (90 G/3¼ OZ) FRESH BREADCRUMBS

¼ CUP (60 ML/2 FL OZ) OLIVE OIL, PLUS EXTRA
    FOR DRIZZLING

2 TABLESPOONS FINELY CHOPPED FLAT-LEAF
    (ITALIAN) PARSLEY

1 TABLESPOON FINELY CHOPPED OREGANO
    LEAVES

2 x 600 G (1 LB 5 OZ) LAMB RACKS, EACH WITH
    EIGHT BONES, FRENCH TRIMMED (ASK YOUR
    BUTCHER TO DO THIS)

To make the olive crust, place the olives, garlic, capers, anchovy fillets and lemon zest in a food processor and process until finely chopped. Transfer to a medium-sized bowl, add the breadcrumbs, olive oil, parsley and oregano and stir well to combine; season with freshly ground black pepper.

Preheat a gas barbecue with a lid to 200°C (400°F). All the burners should be set to medium. Drizzle the lamb racks with olive oil and season with sea salt and pepper. Grill the racks, meat side down, for 2–4 minutes, turning frequently until brown all over.

Transfer the meat to a roasting tray and pack the prepared olive crust over the top of the lamb racks, pressing firmly so that the crust adheres to the meat. Insert a meat thermometer into the centre of the rack. Place the tray in the centre of the grill and turn off the burners directly underneath. Close the lid and cook for 20 minutes for medium–rare, or until the thermometer reads 55°C (131°F).

Remove the tray from the barbecue, cover with foil and set aside to rest for 15 minutes. Cut into slices and serve with Grilled Witlof and Tomato (page 145) and Salt-baked Potatoes (page 128).

SERVES 4

MOQUECA COM PIRAO

SEAFOOD COCONUT STEW WITH MANIOC PASTE

Moqueca has an Afro-Brazilian influence, originating from the north-eastern state of Bahia. Its African influence can be seen with the addition of coconut milk and dendè oil. *Moqueca*, although not a grilled dish, can accompany a selection of grilled sides and starters for a South American–style celebration. It is served here with *pirao*, a tasty gravy made from the *moqueca's* flavoursome stock and thickened with manioc flour.

2 KG (4 LB 6 OZ) WHOLE SNAPPER OR KINGFISH, CLEANED AND SCALED, CUT INTO 2.5 CM (1 INCH) THICK STEAKS

JUICE OF 2 LEMONS

4 GARLIC CLOVES, CRUSHED

2 TEASPOONS SEA SALT

300 G (10½ OZ) DRIED SHRIMP

400 ML (13 FL OZ) TINNED COCONUT MILK

2½ CUPS (625 ML/21 FL OZ) FISH STOCK

3 LARGE BROWN ONIONS, SLICED INTO 1.5 CM (½ INCH) THICK ROUNDS

5 TOMATOES, SLICED INTO 1.5 CM (½ INCH) THICK ROUNDS

½ GREEN CAPSICUM (PEPPER), SEEDED AND SLICED INTO 1.5 CM (½ INCH) THICK ROUNDS

½ YELLOW CAPSICUM (PEPPER), SEEDED AND SLICED INTO 1.5 CM (½ INCH) THICK ROUNDS

½ RED CAPSICUM (PEPPER), SEEDED AND SLICED INTO 1.5 CM (½ INCH) THICK ROUNDS

800 G (1 LB 12 OZ) RAW PRAWNS, PEELED, DEVEINED AND TAILS REMOVED

1 CUP (80 ML/3 FL OZ) DENDÈ OIL (SEE NOTE)

1 LONG RED CHILLI, THINLY SLICED

2 LARGE HANDFULS CORIANDER (CILANTRO) LEAVES, CHOPPED

250 G (9 OZ) MANIOC (CASSAVA) FLOUR

To make the *moqueca*, place the fish steaks in a non-reactive bowl. Add the lemon juice, garlic and sea salt and toss to coat. Cover and leave to marinate in the refrigerator for 30 minutes.

Place the dried shrimp in a food processor and process until finely chopped. Add the coconut milk and blend to combine. Transfer to a medium-sized saucepan over low heat and add the stock.

Arrange half of the onion, tomato and capsicum in layers in the base of a large cast-iron or heavy-based saucepan. Arrange the fish steaks and prawns over the top and pour over the marinade. Arrange the remaining onion, tomato and capsicum in another layer over the top and pour over the heated stock mixture and dendè oil. Sprinkle the chilli and coriander over the top, set the pan over medium heat and bring to the boil. Reduce the heat to low, cover, and cook for 10 minutes, or until the fish flakes easily and the prawns have changed colour. Season with sea salt and freshly ground black pepper. Keep warm until ready to serve.

To make the *pirao*, transfer 1¾ cups (430 ml/14½ fl oz) of the moqueca liquid into a separate saucepan. Stir in the manioc flour to make a thick gravy-like paste. If the mixture is too runny, continue cooking over low heat for 2–3 minutes, or add a little water if it is too thick.

Serve the moqueca with the *pirao* and Brazilian Rice (page 122).

NOTE: Dendè oil is an African oil made from the fruit of the palm tree. It is high in carotene and bright orange in colour. It can be sourced from specialist Latin American, African and Middle Eastern food stores. It creates the characteristic yellow colour of the moqueca.

SERVES 12

SEAFOOD COCONUT STEW WITH MANIOC PASTE

POROTOS GRANADOS

PUMPKIN, CORN AND BORLOTTI BEAN STEW

Traditionally a dish for peasants in Chile who were working the land, this hearty, lightly spiced stew is sure to appeal to vegetarians and meat lovers alike. The pumpkin and corn give the stew a creamy texture and slightly sweet flavour. It is perfect teamed with rice or crusty bread, they're ideal for soaking up the flavoursome juices.

2 TABLESPOONS VEGETABLE OIL

I ONION, CHOPPED

3 GARLIC CLOVES, FINELY CHOPPED

2 TEASPOONS PAPRIKA

I TEASPOON GROUND CUMIN

I TEASPOON DRIED OREGANO

4 CUPS (I LITRE/34 FL OZ) VEGETABLE STOCK

250 G (9 OZ/1¼ CUPS) BORLOTTI BEANS,
    SOAKED IN COLD WATER OVERNIGHT
    AND DRAINED

2 COBS SWEET CORN

500 G (I LB 2 OZ) PUMPKIN, PEELED, SEEDED
    AND CUT INTO 2.5 CM (I INCH) CHUNKS

I HANDFUL BASIL LEAVES

Heat the vegetable oil in a saucepan over low–medium heat. Cook the onion and garlic until softened. Add the paprika, cumin and oregano and cook until fragrant. Pour in the vegetable stock and bring to the boil. Add the borlotti beans, reduce the heat, and simmer for 30–40 minutes, or until the beans are almost tender.

Grate the corn into a bowl, reserving any juices. Add the pumpkin, corn and its juice to the stew and stir to combine. Simmer for a further 20–25 minutes, or until the pumpkin is tender. Season with sea salt and freshly ground black pepper.

Serve the stew topped with basil leaves, and steamed rice or fresh crusty bread to accompany.

SERVES 4

ESPETINHO DE FRANGO COM CACHAÇA E LIMÃO

CACHAÇA AND LIME CHICKEN SKEWERS

Cachaça is one of the most popular alcoholic drinks in Brazil, made from fresh sugar cane juice that is first fermented, then distilled. As well as being one of the base ingredients for making caipirinhas, the well-known cocktail (page 193), it can also be used as it is here to marinate these delicious chicken skewers, which helps to keep the meat moist. Use vodka if *cachaça* is unavailable.

8 BAMBOO SKEWERS

¼ CUP (60 ML/2 FL OZ) CACHAÇA

FINELY GRATED ZEST AND JUICE OF 1 LIME

1 SMALL HANDFUL CORIANDER (CILANTRO)
    LEAVES, FINELY CHOPPED

1 LONG GREEN CHILLI, SEEDED AND FINELY
    CHOPPED

2 TABLESPOONS OLIVE OIL

1 TABLESPOON HONEY

1 GARLIC CLOVE, CRUSHED

1 TEASPOON SEA SALT

3 SKINLESS CHICKEN BREAST FILLETS, CUT
    INTO 2.5 CM (1 INCH) CUBES

VEGETABLE OIL, FOR BRUSHING

Soak the bamboo skewers in cold water for 30 minutes to prevent them from burning during cooking.

Combine all of the ingredients, except the chicken and vegetable oil, in a non-reactive bowl. Add the chicken and toss to coat. Cover and leave to marinate in the refrigerator for 1–2 hours.

Thread the chicken onto the skewers, approximately four pieces on each skewer.

Preheat a barbecue chargrill to medium. Brush a little vegetable oil over the chargrill and cook the chicken skewers for 6–8 minutes, turning occasionally, until cooked through and lightly charred. Serve with Quinoa Salad (page 140) and Grilled Corn (page 142).

MAKES 8

FRIDAY NIGHTS WITH YOUR MATES

SERVES 6

DAY BEFORE:

- Marinate Pork Ribs
- Prepare Brazilian Passionfruit Mousse, cover and refrigerate

DAY OF:

- Make Pebre, cover and refrigerate
- Prepare *Cheiro Verde* Sauce, cover and refrigerate
- Prepare Quinoa Salad, but do not dress, cover and refrigerate
- Prepare Corn, but do not cook

30 MINUTES BEFORE GUESTS ARRIVE:

- Preheat the barbecue
- Put Pork Ribs on to cook
- Set up bar for making Pisco Sours

UPON GUESTS' ARRIVAL:

- Make Pisco Sours and serve
- Grill and serve Mozzarella with *Cheiro Verde* Sauce
- Cook Chorizo, slice and serve
- Check Pork Ribs and when cooked, remove and set aside to rest
- Grill Corn while the ribs are resting
- Slice and serve Pork Ribs with Grilled Corn, Quinoa Salad and Pebre
- Serve Brazilian Passionfruit Mousse when ready

COSTELETAS DE PORCO

PORK RIBS

Pork ribs are commonly cooked in Brazil. Here they are cooked slowly in foil, keeping them beautifully moist and tender with crisp crackling the much desired prize for most pork lovers. They are a great addition to any barbecue and once marinated require little more than a single turn on the grill, leaving you more time to enjoy with your friends and family.

2.5 KG (5½ LB) WHOLE PORK RIBS

JUICE OF 1 LEMON

2 TABLESPOONS OLIVE OIL

1 SMALL HANDFUL OREGANO LEAVES,
　CHOPPED

3 GARLIC CLOVES, CRUSHED

2 TABLESPOONS SEA SALT

VEGETABLE OIL, FOR GREASING

LEMON WEDGES, TO SERVE (OPTIONAL)

Remove and discard the thin membrane from the bone side of the ribs. Score the fat, using a sharp knife to make a criss-cross pattern.

Combine the lemon juice, olive oil, oregano, garlic and half of the salt in a small bowl. Rub the mixture over the ribs to coat, place on a large non-reactive tray, cover, and refrigerate for at least 2 hours or overnight.

Preheat a barbecue chargrill to low–medium. Remove the ribs from the refrigerator and rub the remaining salt over the skin. Cut a double layer of foil large enough to wrap the ribs. Wrap the ribs in both layers to completely enclose. Grill the ribs, bone side down, for 1½ hours.

Turn the ribs over and grill for a further 45–60 minutes, or until the fat is crisp and golden brown and the meat is tender. Remove from the heat and set the ribs aside to rest for 15 minutes.

Just before you are ready to serve, unwrap the meat, transfer to a chopping board and slice between the bones. Squeeze the lemon wedges over before serving, if desired. These pork ribs go well with the Brazilian Potato Salad (page 148).

SERVES 6

MATAMBRE AROLLADO

ROLLED BEEF STUFFED WITH EGG AND VEGETABLES

Matambre arollado is made using skirt steak (*matambre*). This quick-to-cook cut, which translates to 'hunger killer' in Argentina, is commonly cooked, sliced and shared at the beginning of an *asado*, helping to keep people's hunger at bay while they wait for larger cuts of meat to cook. Here it is rolled and stuffed with brightly coloured vegetables and boiled eggs to make an impressive looking dish which is more of a main event. It can be prepared in advance, which makes it a good choice for entertaining.

1 LARGE CARROT, PEELED AND CUT LENGTHWISE INTO 1 CM (½ INCH) THICK STRIPS

1 BUNCH ENGLISH SPINACH, WASHED AND DRAINED

1.5 KG (3 LB 5 OZ) SKIRT STEAK, BUTTERFLIED (ABOUT 3 x 500 G/1 LB 2 OZ PIECES)

3 GARLIC CLOVES, FINELY CHOPPED

1 SMALL HANDFUL OREGANO LEAVES, CHOPPED

4 LARGE HARD-BOILED EGGS, PEELED

1 QUANTITY GRILLED RED CAPSICUM (PEPPER), CUT LENGTHWISE INTO 1 CM (½ INCH) THICK STRIPS (PAGE 138)

OLIVE OIL, FOR DRIZZLING

Bring a large saucepan of water to the boil. Cook the carrot for 2 minutes, or until tender. Remove using a slotted spoon and set aside. Blanch the spinach for 10 seconds, or until wilted. Drain and refresh immediately in iced water to stop the cooking process. Drain and spread out on a clean tea towel or use paper towels to remove any excess moisture.

Cover a clean work surface with enough plastic wrap to lay out the steak. Arrange the steak pieces so they are overlapping slightly, cut side up, to make one large rectangular piece of meat. Turn the meat so the shortest side is facing you. Sprinkle with the garlic and oregano and season with sea salt and freshly ground black pepper.

Arrange the open spinach leaves across the meat. Visually divide the meat into thirds lengthwise. Arrange the eggs across the middle of the third closest to you, then make a row of carrot and capsicum alongside. Roll the end of the meat over the eggs and vegetables to firmly enclose. Continue rolling down the entire length of the meat to create a thick roll. Tie with kitchen string to secure. Season the outside with salt and pepper and drizzle with olive oil.

Preheat a gas barbecue with a lid to 180°C (350°F). All the burners should be set to medium.

Place the meat, seam side down, on the barbecue, close the lid and cook for 20–25 minutes for medium, or until cooked to your liking, turning occasionally to ensure it is cooked evenly on all sides. Transfer to a baking tray, cover with foil, and set aside to rest for 5 minutes.

To serve, remove the kitchen string and cut the meat into 3 cm (1¼ inch) thick rounds. This dish is best served with a simple green salad.

SERVES 8–10

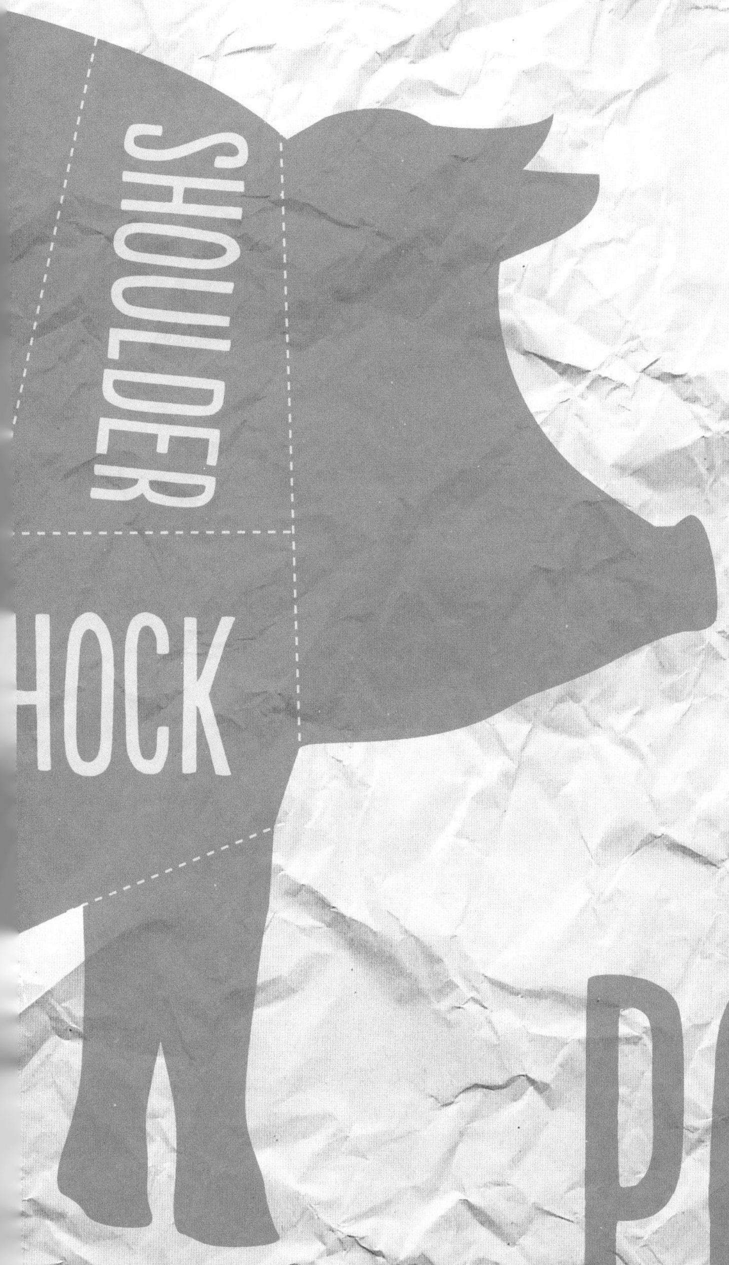

PORK

ESPETINHO DE PEIXE

BRAZILIAN FISH SKEWERS

Firm oily fish such as tuna or salmon can be used to make these skewers, as they can take the high temperatures of the grill while their strong flavours are complemented with subtle charring. Quick to cook, they make a great start to a procession of mains when planning a South American feast.

8 BAMBOO SKEWERS

¼ CUP (60 ML/2 FL OZ) DRY WHITE WINE

JUICE OF 1 LEMON

2 TABLESPOONS OLIVE OIL

1 GARLIC CLOVE, CRUSHED

2 TEASPOONS SEA SALT

600 G (1 LB 5 OZ) TUNA OR SALMON FILLETS, CUT INTO 3 CM (1¼ INCH) CUBES

1 RED CAPSICUM (PEPPER), SEEDED AND CUT INTO 3 CM (1¼ INCH) PIECES

1 GREEN CAPSICUM (PEPPER), SEEDED AND CUT INTO 3 CM (1¼ INCH) PIECES

1 LARGE RED ONION, CUT INTO 3 CM (1¼ INCH) PIECES

VEGETABLE OIL, FOR BRUSHING

Soak the bamboo skewers in cold water for 30 minutes to prevent them from burning during cooking.

Put the white wine, lemon juice, olive oil, garlic and salt into a non-reactive bowl and stir to combine. Add the fish and toss to coat. Cover and leave to marinate in the refrigerator for 30 minutes.

Thread the fish, capsicum and onion alternately onto the pre-soaked skewers.

Preheat a barbecue chargrill to medium–high. Brush a little vegetable oil over the chargrill and cook the skewers for 6 minutes, turning frequently, or until lightly charred and the fish is just cooked through.

Serve with Palm Heart Salad (page 126) and Argentinian Grilled Garlic and Rosemary Flat Bread (page 155).

MAKES 8

ASADO NEGRO

'BLACK ROAST' VENEZUELAN SUGAR-CRUSTED BEEF

Asado negro is the signature dish of Venezuela's capital, Caracas. It is traditionally slow-roasted in the oven, but has been adapted here to make it suitable for the barbecue. The sugar, vinegar, worcestershire sauce and garlic marinade creates a sweet, yet balanced, black glaze on the meat once cooked, leaving the centre pink and juicy.

1 CUP (185 G/6½ OZ) SOFT BROWN SUGAR

1 CUP (80 ML/3 FL OZ) WHITE WINE VINEGAR

¼ CUP (60 ML/2 FL OZ) WORCESTERSHIRE SAUCE

6 GARLIC CLOVES, CRUSHED

½ TEASPOON FRESHLY GROUND BLACK PEPPER

2 KG (4 LB 6 OZ) WHOLE SCOTCH FILLET

Combine the sugar, vinegar, worcestershire sauce, garlic and pepper in a medium-sized bowl.

Place the scotch fillet in a roasting tray, coat in the sugar mixture, cover and leave to marinate in the refrigerator for 2–4 hours.

Preheat a gas barbecue with a lid to 180°C (350°F). All the burners should be set to medium.

Remove the meat from the refrigerator and allow it to come to room temperature, then transfer the fillet to a large roasting tray and insert a meat thermometer into the centre of the meat. Place the tray in the centre of the barbecue and turn off the burners directly underneath. Cover and cook for 1 hour for medium–rare, basting occasionally with the remaining marinade, until the meat thermometer reads 55°C (131°F).

Remove the tray from the barbecue, cover the meat with foil and set aside to rest for 15 minutes. Cut the scotch fillet into slices and serve with steamed rice and Grilled Plantain in Breadcrumbs (page 141).

SERVES 8

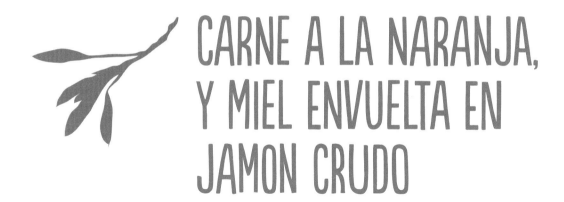

CARNE A LA NARANJA, Y MIEL ENVUELTA EN JAMON CRUDO

PORK WRAPPED IN PROSCIUTTO WITH ORANGE AND HONEY

Reflecting Argentina's Italian influence, this dish is inspired by *saltimbocca* — veal steak with sage, wrapped in prosciutto. Here, a contrast of flavours, such as the sweetness of honey and slight tart of orange are used to complement the saltiness of the meat.

4 x 150 G (5 OZ) BONELESS PORK LOIN STEAKS

8 SAGE LEAVES

1 ORANGE, PEELED AND THINLY SLICED INTO
   ROUNDS

2 TABLESPOONS HONEY

8 THIN SLICES PROSCIUTTO

VEGETABLE OIL, FOR BRUSHING

Preheat a barbecue chargrill or hotplate to medium–high.

Remove and discard the skin from the steaks. Season the pork with sea salt and freshly ground black pepper. Lay two sage leaves on each piece of pork, top with two slices of orange and drizzle with a little honey. Wrap each piece of pork in two slices of prosciutto, tucking the ends underneath.

Brush a little vegetable oil over the grill. Cook the wrapped pork for 2–3 minutes on each side, or until the prosciutto is crisp and golden brown and the pork is cooked through. Serve with Grilled Red Capsicum (page 138) and Salt-baked Potatoes (page 128).

SERVES 4

POLLO A LA PARRILLA CON LIMON Y ROMERITO

BUTTERFLIED LEMON AND ROSEMARY CHICKEN

Chicken is often butterflied and grilled whole in South America. Cooking in this way aids the meat to cook evenly and helps prevent the delicate breast meat from drying out. The marinade gives the chicken a garlicky tang which perfectly complements the charred and crisp skin. Delicious!

1.5 KG (3 LB 5 OZ) WHOLE FREE-RANGE CHICKEN

3 GARLIC CLOVES, CRUSHED

1 TEASPOON GROUND CUMIN

1 TEASPOON FRESHLY GROUND BLACK PEPPER

2 LEMONS

2 TABLESPOONS OLIVE OIL

1 SMALL HANDFUL ROSEMARY LEAVES

VEGETABLE OIL, FOR GREASING

ROCK SALT, FOR SEASONING

To butterfly the chicken, place it breast side down on a chopping board. Use kitchen scissors or a large sharp knife to cut along both sides of the backbone from the tail to the neck and remove the backbone. Turn the chicken over and use the palm of your hand to press down and break the breastbone. Cut the skin connecting the thighs and the body and bend the thighs outwards to break the joints. The chicken should now lay flat and cook more evenly. Wash under cold running water and pat dry with paper towels.

To make the marinade, mix the garlic, cumin and pepper together in a small bowl to make a smooth paste. Finely grate the zest of one of the lemons and juice both the lemons. Add the lemon zest, lemon juice, olive oil and rosemary to the garlic mixture and stir to combine.

Smear the mixture over the bone side of the chicken and under the skin of the chicken breast. Place on a large non-reactive tray, cover, and leave to marinate in the refrigerator for 2–4 hours.

Preheat a charcoal or gas barbecue to 180°C (350°F). All the burners should be set to medium. Brush a little vegetable oil over the grill.

Season the chicken with rock salt and cook the chicken, breast side down, for 15 minutes, or until the skin is golden brown and crisp. Turn the chicken over, close the barbecue lid and cook for a further 15–20 minutes, or until the juices run clear when a skewer is inserted into the thickest part of the thigh. Transfer to a chopping board, cover with foil, and leave to rest for 5 minutes.

To serve, cut the chicken into eight pieces and serve with Quinoa Salad (page 140).

SERVES 4

TRUTA GRELHADA COM VINAGRETE

BUTTERFLIED TROUT WITH VINAGRETE

Removing the backbone and bones from the trout may take a little time and practice but it is worth the effort — it makes the eating more pleasurable as the skin is cooked to crisp on one side while the pink flesh is topped with a fresh Brazilian salsa, imparting flavour and colour, and keeping the fish lovely and moist.

2 x 300 G (10½ OZ) WHOLE RAINBOW TROUT, CLEANED AND SCALED

OLIVE OIL, FOR DRIZZLING

1 CUP (250 ML/8½ FL OZ) VINAGRETE (PAGE 115)

LEMON WEDGES, TO SERVE

To butterfly the trout, slip the blade of a thin sharp knife under one side of the ribs and slice down the backbone to the tip of the tail. Take care not to go all the way through as you want to keep the two fillets joined at the bottom and the skin intact. Keep your blade as close to the bone as possible, so you don't lose too much meat. Repeat on the other side of the ribs. Use kitchen scissors to cut the backbone away from the tail. Gently pull the backbone up towards the head of the fish. Cut the backbone away from the head and discard both. The fish should now lay flat.

Preheat a barbecue chargrill to medium–high. Rub a little olive oil over the skin of the fish and season both sides with sea salt and freshly ground black pepper. Place the fish, skin side down, on a closable wire fish barbecue rack, if you have one. Scatter the *vinagrete* over the flesh of the fish and fasten the grill shut. Alternatively, place the fish, skin side down on a double sheet of foil and scatter with the *vinagrete*.

Grill the fish, skin side down, either using the fish rack or in the foil for 10–12 minutes without turning, or until the skin is crisp and the flesh is just cooked through. Transfer to a serving plate and serve with lemon wedges and either the Brazilian Rice (page 122) and Palm Heart Salad (page 126) or Salt-baked Potatoes (page 128) and Grilled Corn Three Ways (page 142).

SERVES 2

PEIXE ASSADO RECHEADO COM FAROFA

WHOLE FISH STUFFED WITH FAROFA

Farofa is made from toasted manioc (cassava) flour. It is used in this dish as a stuffing for the fish, adding an interesting textural element and soaking up the cooking juices. *Farofa pronto* is a pre-seasoned 'ready to eat' version which can be purchased from Latin American food stores or online. It is a great time-saving alternative, just keep a bag of it handy in your cupboard and you're good to go. Alternatively, toast your own as per the recipe on page 120.

1. 5 KG (3 LB 5 OZ) WHOLE SNAPPER, BARRAMUNDI OR WHITING, CLEANED AND SCALED, HEAD LEFT ON

JUICE OF 3 LEMONS

2 TABLESPOONS OLIVE OIL

FAROFA PRONTO (PRE-SEASONED AND TOASTED MANIOC FLOUR) OR TOASTED FAROFA, FOR STUFFING

VINAGRETE (PAGE 115), TO SERVE

Place the fish on a non-reactive tray, pour over the lemon juice, drizzle with the olive oil and season with sea salt and freshly ground black pepper, including inside the cavity. Cover and leave to marinate in the refrigerator for 30 minutes.

Cut a double layer of foil large enough to wrap the fish. Remove the fish from the marinade, place on the foil and stuff the cavity with *farofa*. Wrap the fish in the double layer of foil and seal to enclose. Place the fish on a closable wire fish barbecue grill, if you have one, and fasten shut.

Preheat a barbecue chargrill to medium—high. Grill the fish for 6—8 minutes on each side, then remove from the heat and set aside to rest for 5 minutes.

To serve, open up the parcel and gently lift out the fish and place on a serving plate. Serve with the leftover *farofa* and the vinagrete.

SERVES 4

MILANESA DE TERNERO

CRUMBED VEAL STEAKS

A German classic, this version was adopted by the Italians (the title translates as 'in the style of Milan'), and is commonly found in Argentinian restaurants. Essentially it is a thin slice of meat (it can also be made using beef, pork or chicken) which is breaded and shallow-fried. Traditionally, it is cooked in a frying pan but also develops a lovely crisp coating when cooked on the barbecue. Serve with Brazilian Potato Salad (page 148).

¾ CUP (110 G/4 OZ) PLAIN (ALL-PURPOSE) FLOUR

4 CUPS (250 G/9 OZ) FRESH BREADCRUMBS

1 HANDFUL FLAT-LEAF (ITALIAN) PARSLEY, CHOPPED

8 VEAL STEAKS, ABOUT 1 CM (½ INCH) THICK

3 LARGE EGGS, LIGHTLY BEATEN

¼ CUP (60 ML/2 FL OZ) OLIVE OIL

60 G (2 OZ) BUTTER

LEMON WEDGES, TO SERVE

Place the flour on a large plate and season with sea salt and freshly ground black pepper. In a separate bowl, combine the breadcrumbs and parsley.

Coat the veal steaks first in the flour, then in the egg and finally in the breadcrumb mixture, pressing lightly to coat each steak.

Preheat a barbecue chargrill or hotplate to medium–high.

Heat the olive oil and butter together in a small saucepan, until the butter has melted. Brush the chargrill with half of the oil mixture. Cook the crumbed steaks on one side for 3–4 minutes, or until golden-brown. Drizzle the remaining oil mixture on top of the steaks, turn and cook for a further 3–4 minutes, or until golden brown. Drain off any excess oil using paper towels and serve hot with lemon wedges for squeezing over and Brazilian Potato Salad on the side.

SERVES 4

HORNADO DE CHANCHO

MARINATED ROAST PORK LEG

This recipe needs to be prepared two days in advance but it is well worth the effort. All that is required is to juice some limes, make a simple spiced garlic marinade and coat the pork, then the following day marinate it in beer. After that, you just need to cook it — easy!

4.5 KG (9 LB 14 OZ) PORK LEG, BONED AND
   ROLLED (ASK YOUR BUTCHER TO DO THIS
   FOR YOU)

18 GARLIC CLOVES, CRUSHED

2 TABLESPOONS GROUND CUMIN

2 TABLESPOONS SEA SALT

1½ TABLESPOONS PAPRIKA

2 TEASPOONS FRESHLY GROUND
   BLACK PEPPER

JUICE OF 4 LIMES

3 x 375 ML (12½ FL OZ) BOTTLES BEER (LAGER)

80 G (3 OZ) BUTTER, MELTED

Use a small sharp knife to score the skin of the pork and make several deep incisions in the pork leg. Place in a non-reactive tray.

Combine the garlic, cumin, salt, paprika and pepper in a bowl.

Pour the lime juice over the pork and rub into all sides, then rub the spiced garlic paste over the pork, pushing it into the incisions. Cover and leave to marinate in the refrigerator for 12–24 hours.

Pour the beer over the pork, cover and return to the refrigerator to marinate for a further 12–24 hours, turning occasionally so that the leg marinates evenly.

Preheat a gas barbecue fitted with a rotisserie to 200°C (400°F). All the burners should be turned to medium. Insert the rotisserie rod lengthwise through the leg of pork, ensuring the pork leg is evenly balanced. Secure the rotisserie spit according to the manufacturer's instructions. Turn off the burners directly underneath the pork, leaving the side burners on medium. Place a drip tray filled with 1 cm (½ inch) water underneath the pork.

Baste the pork with the melted butter. Reduce the heat to 180°C (350°F) and cook the pork for 1½–2 hours, or until the skin is crisp and golden brown and the meat is just cooked through — test with a skewer, the juices should run clear.

Use barbecue mitts to carefully remove the rotisserie rod. Take the pork off the rod and place on a large tray. Cover with foil and set aside to rest for 10 minutes. Cut into slices and serve with Peruvian Onion Salsa (page 110), Brazilian Rice (page 122) and Grilled Red Capsicum (page 138).

SERVES 12

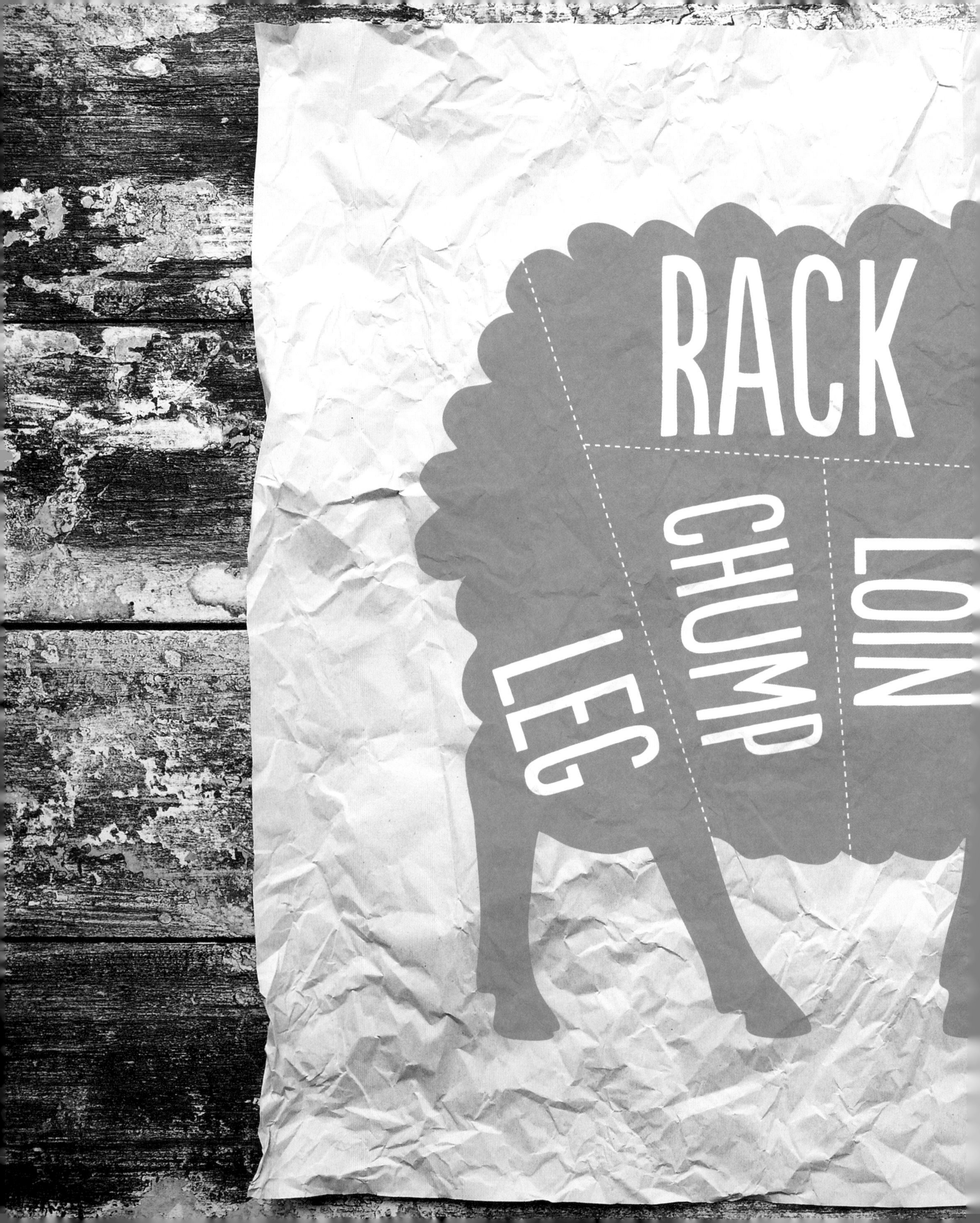

RACK
LOIN
CHUMP
LEG

NECK

SHOULDER

SHANK

LAMB

PAMPLONA DE POLLO

ROLLED STUFFED CHICKEN BREAST

Traditionally, caul fat is used to make this popular dish from Uruguay. Caul fat is the thin lacy membrane of fat, which lines the internal organs of an animal — it doesn't impart much flavour but it is edible and does help to keep the chicken moist during cooking. Pork caul fat is most commonly used and can be sourced from most good butchers. Use kitchen string if caul fat is unavailable.

4 SKINLESS CHICKEN BREAST FILLETS

4 SLICES SMOKED HAM

2 GRILLED RED CAPSICUMS (PEPPERS),
    SLICED INTO THICK STRIPS (PAGE 138)

150 G (5 OZ) MOZZARELLA CHEESE, CUT
    INTO THICK STRIPS

250 G (9 OZ) CAUL FAT (OR USE KITCHEN
    STRING IF UNAVAILABLE)

VEGETABLE OIL, FOR BRUSHING

Use a sharp knife to butterfly the thickest part of each chicken breast, cutting the breast horizontally almost all the way through, so the breast folds out in an even thickness. Place the butterflied chicken breasts between two sheets of baking paper and use a meat mallet to pound them out and flatten slightly. Season with sea salt and freshly ground black pepper.

Place each chicken breast, smooth side down, on a clean work surface. Lay a slice of ham on top of each chicken breast and lay strips of capsicum and mozzarella lengthwise down the centre. Fold and roll the chicken breast to enclose the filling.

Cut the caul fat into four large rectangular pieces, large enough to wrap the chicken parcels. Wrap the chicken in the caul fat with the edges coming together at the base of the roll. Trim the caul fat as needed. Alternatively, use kitchen string to tie them securely.

Preheat a barbecue chargrill or hotplate to medium. Brush a little vegetable oil over the chargrill and cook the chicken for 20–25 minutes, turning occasionally, until golden brown and cooked through.

If you have used kitchen string, remove it now. Cut each chicken breast into slices and serve with Lima Bean Salad (page 144).

SERVES 4

SALCHICHAS

SOUTH AMERICAN SAUSAGES

At South American barbecues a selection of sausages is often served at the beginning of the meal as they are quick to cook and ready well before larger cuts of meat. They are usually sliced and shared between guests to curb their hunger and get the digestive juices flowing. Morcilla is the Spanish version of the Scottish black pudding — it is a richly spiced boiled sausage made using pig's blood. Linguica is a Portuguese smoked sausage, while chorizo, heavily spiced with paprika, is a popular Spanish-style sausage.

6 CHORIZO SAUSAGES

24 SMALL OR 12 LARGE LINGUICA
   (PORTUGUESE SMOKED PORK SAUSAGES)

4 MORCILLA (BLOOD SAUSAGES)

2 LONG METAL BARBECUE SKEWERS
   (OPTIONAL)

SALSA PICANTE (CHILLI SALSA)

8 LONG RED CHILLIES, SEEDED AND CHOPPED

2 TOMATOES, PEELED AND CHOPPED

2 GARLIC CLOVES, CHOPPED

1 TABLESPOON EXTRA-VIRGIN OLIVE OIL, PLUS
   EXTRA FOR STORING

JUICE OF 1 LIME

To make the *salsa picante*, put the chilli, tomato and garlic into a food processor and process to make a smooth sauce.

Heat the olive oil in a large frying pan over low–medium heat. Add the chilli sauce and cook, stirring, for 10 minutes, or until thickened. Remove from the heat, stir in the lime juice and season with sea salt. Transfer to a serving bowl and set aside until ready to serve.

Preheat a barbecue chargrill to medium.

Thread three chorizo sausages onto each skewer, piercing through the middle of each sausage. Separate them slightly so there is a small gap between each sausage to aid even cooking.

Cook the chorizo and linguica sausages for 15–20 minutes, turning occasionally, until the skin is crisp and brown and the sausages are cooked through. Add the morcilla sausages — these will only take 10 minutes to heat through.

Pull the chorizo off the skewer. Slice the chorizo and morcilla sausages and serve them all with the *salsa picante* on the side with Brazilian Potato Salad (page 148) and Grilled Corn (page 142).

Any leftover salsa can be stored in an airtight container, covered with a thin layer of oil. Store in the refrigerator for up to 2 weeks.

SERVES 12

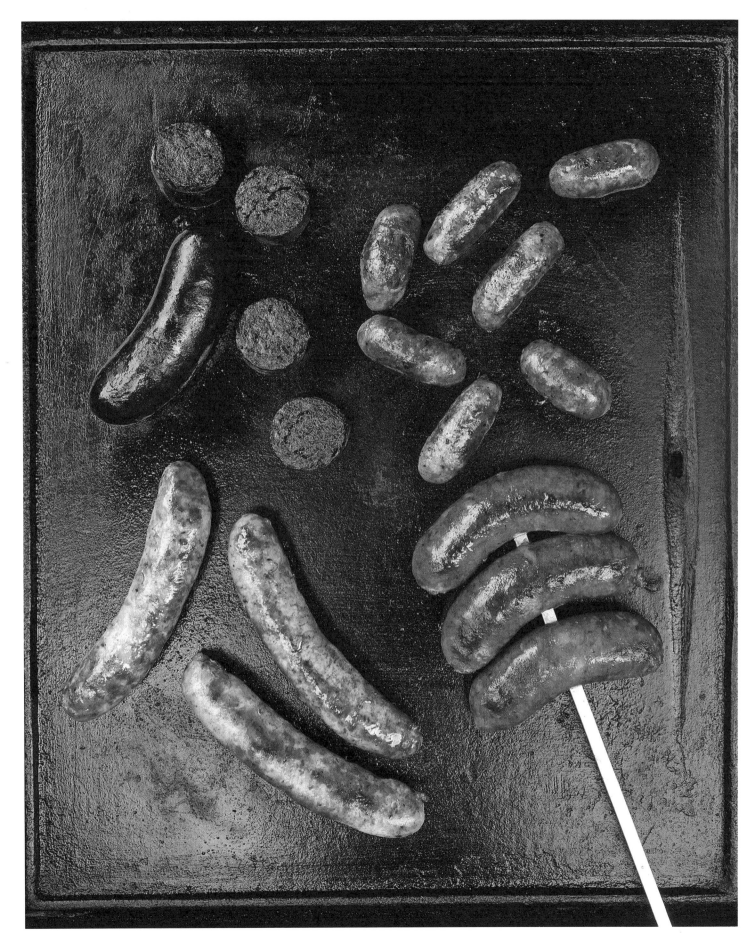

MEJILLONES CON HIERBAS Y AJO

MUSSELS WITH GARLIC AND HERBS

Due to its long coastline, seafood is abundant in Chile and its use is prevalent, particularly in stews. In this dish, mussels are steamed (enclosed in foil) on the barbecue and topped with a simple combination of herbs and wine allowing their delicate flavour to shine through.

2 KG (4 LB 6 OZ) BLACK MUSSELS, SCRUBBED
   AND DE-BEARDED
4 GARLIC CLOVES, CRUSHED
3 SPRING ONIONS (SCALLIONS), THINLY SLICED
2 LARGE HANDFULS FLAT-LEAF (ITALIAN)
   PARSLEY, CHOPPED
¼ CUP (60 ML/2 FL OZ) DRY WHITE WINE
¼ CUP (60 ML/2 FL OZ) EXTRA-VIRGIN
   OLIVE OIL

Preheat a barbecue chargrill or hotplate to medium–high.

Cut two double layers of aluminium foil large enough to enclose the mussels in two parcels. Divide the mussels in half and place on the centre of the foil pieces. Sprinkle with the garlic, spring onion and parsley. Drizzle with the white wine and olive oil.
Draw up the sides of the foil and fold over the edges to seal and create two airtight packages.

Place the wrapped mussels on the chargrill and cook for 10–15 minutes, or until all the mussels have opened. Unwrap the mussels and transfer to a large serving bowl to eat straight away. Serve with crusty bread.

SERVES 4

POLLO A LA BRASA

PERUVIAN ROTISSERIE CHICKEN

Traditionally cooked on a rotisserie over hot coals and served with chips, these chickens are marinated in a garlic herb paste, infusing the meat with flavour. Popular throughout Peru, this dish has been the inspiration behind many a barbecue chicken shop in the West. After making this version, you'll never go out for chicken again.

2 x 1.5 KG (3 LB 5 OZ) WHOLE FREE-RANGE
  CHICKENS

8 GARLIC CLOVES, CHOPPED

2 CM (¾ INCH) PIECE GINGER, PEELED AND
  CHOPPED

2 TABLESPOONS DRIED OREGANO

1 TABLESPOON GROUND CUMIN

1 TABLESPOON PAPRIKA

1 TABLESPOON SEA SALT

2 TEASPOONS FRESHLY GROUND BLACK
  PEPPER

½ CUP (125 ML/4 FL OZ) WHITE VINEGAR

Rinse the chickens under cold running water, cleaning out the inside cavities. Pat dry, trim any excess fat and tuck in the wings.

Combine the garlic, ginger, oregano, cumin, paprika, salt and pepper in a food processor and process to make a smooth paste. Add the vinegar and process to combine.

Place the chickens on a non-reactive tray. Coat the chickens in the spice mixture, rubbing it under the skin and inside the cavities. Cover and marinate in the refrigerator for at least 4 hours or overnight.

Preheat a gas barbecue fitted with a rotisserie to 200°C (400°F). All of the burners should be set to medium. Insert the rotisserie rod through the cavities of the chickens and centre them on the rod. Secure the rotisserie according to the manufacturer's instructions. Turn off the burners directly underneath the chickens, leaving the side burners on medium. Place a drip tray filled with 1 cm (½ inch) water underneath the chickens.

Cook the chickens for 1–1¼ hours, or until crisp and golden brown and the juices run clear when a skewer is inserted into the thickest part of the thigh. Wearing barbecue mitts, carefully remove the rotisserie rod. Take the chickens off the rod and place on a large tray. Cover with foil and set aside to rest for 10 minutes. Carve the chickens into quarters or eight pieces, to serve.

SERVES 8

PERUVIAN ROTISSERIE CHICKEN

SAUCES AND SALSAS

CHIMICHURRI

ARGENTINIAN GREEN SAUCE

This is the quintessential condiment in Argentina, traditionally used as a marinade or as a sauce for grilled red meats, although it is quite versatile and works well with chicken and fish dishes as well.

5 GARLIC CLOVES, CRUSHED

2 TEASPOONS SEA SALT

1 TEASPOON DRIED CHILLI FLAKES

½ TEASPOON PAPRIKA

½ TEASPOON FRESHLY GROUND
   BLACK PEPPER

¼ RED ONION, FINELY CHOPPED

3 LARGE HANDFULS FLAT-LEAF (ITALIAN)
   PARSLEY, FINELY CHOPPED

1 SMALL HANDFUL OREGANO LEAVES,
   FINELY CHOPPED

2 TABLESPOONS RED WINE VINEGAR

2 TABLESPOONS LEMON JUICE

1 CUP (80 ML/3 FL OZ) EXTRA-VIRGIN
   OLIVE OIL

Put the garlic, salt, chilli flakes, paprika and pepper into a medium-sized bowl and stir to make a smooth paste. Add the onion, parsley, oregano, vinegar, lemon juice and olive oil and stir to combine. Cover with plastic wrap and refrigerate for at least 1 hour, to allow the flavours to infuse.

Any leftover sauce can be stored in an airtight container in the refrigerator for up to 5 days.

MAKES 1 CUP

SALSA CRIOLLA
PERUVIAN ONION SALSA

This Peruvian salsa has a combination of subtle sweetness from the red onion and capsicum and a vibrant tang from the lime juice to provide a perfect contrast to grilled meats, chicken and fish.

2 LARGE RED ONIONS, THINLY SLICED

I RED CAPSICUM (PEPPER), SEEDED AND
    THINLY SLICED INTO 4 CM (1½ INCH) STRIPS

I LARGE HANDFUL FRESH FLAT-LEAF (ITALIAN)
    PARSLEY, CHOPPED

¼ CUP (60 ML/2 FL OZ) LIME JUICE

I CUP (80 ML/3 FL OZ) EXTRA-VIRGIN
    OLIVE OIL

Combine the onion, capsicum and parsley in a medium-sized bowl. Add the lime juice and olive oil and stir to combine. Season with sea salt and freshly ground black pepper, to taste. Transfer to a small serving bowl.

Any leftover salsa can be stored in an airtight container in the refrigerator for up to 2 days.

MAKES 4 CUPS

PEBRE

TOMATO, CORIANDER AND CHILLI SALSA

This versatile Chilean salsa is a tasty accompaniment to most grilled meats and bread. Perfect for those who prefer a little spice in their meals.

2 ONIONS, FINELY DICED

4 VINE-RIPENED TOMATOES, FINELY DICED

½ GREEN CAPSICUM (PEPPER), SEEDED AND FINELY DICED

3 LARGE HANDFULS CHOPPED CORIANDER (CILANTRO) LEAVES

4 GARLIC CLOVES, FINELY CHOPPED

2 LONG RED CHILLIES, SEEDED AND FINELY DICED

JUICE OF ½ LEMON

2 TABLESPOONS WHITE WINE VINEGAR

2 TABLESPOONS EXTRA-VIRGIN OLIVE OIL

1 TEASPOON SEA SALT

1 TEASPOON DRIED OREGANO

Soak the onion in cold water for 15 minutes, then rinse and drain well — this will help mellow the flavour.

Combine the onion with all of the remaining ingredients, except the oregano, in a medium-sized bowl.

Transfer to a serving dish and sprinkle the oregano over the top. Cover and refrigerate for 2 hours, to allow the flavours to develop.

Serve the salsa as an accompaniment with grilled meat, chicken and fish.

Any leftover salsa can be stored in an airtight container in the refrigerator for up to 2 days.

MAKES 4 CUPS

PEBRE (LEFT) AND SALSA CRIOLLA (RIGHT)

GUASACACA

AVOCADO SAUCE

This is a smooth bright green sauce with a vinegary tang. It is a popular condiment in Venezuela and is most often served with grilled meats, sausage, chicken and fish, or as a sauce for *Arepas de Queso* (page 32).

½ WHITE ONION, ROUGHLY CHOPPED

½ GREEN CAPSICUM (PEPPER), SEEDED AND ROUGHLY CHOPPED

2 GARLIC CLOVES, ROUGHLY CHOPPED

2 AVOCADOS, HALVED LENGTHWISE, STONE REMOVED AND FLESH ROUGHLY CHOPPED

1 LARGE HANDFUL CORIANDER (CILANTRO) LEAVES

1 LARGE HANDFUL FLAT-LEAF (ITALIAN) PARSLEY

1 CUP (80 ML/3 FL OZ) RED WINE VINEGAR

¼ CUP (60 ML/2 FL OZ) EXTRA-VIRGIN OLIVE OIL

Combine the onion, capsicum and garlic in a food processor and process until finely chopped. Add the avocado, coriander, parsley, vinegar and olive oil and continue to process until smooth. Season with sea salt and freshly ground black pepper, to taste.

Transfer to a serving bowl and serve as an accompaniment with grilled meat, chicken and fish.

Any leftover sauce can be stored in an airtight container in the refrigerator for up to 2–3 days — any longer and the avocado will begin to discolour and turn brown.

MAKES 3 CUPS

VINAGRETE

BRAZILIAN SALSA

A must at any Brazilian barbecue, this colourful, piquant salsa is very versatile and can be served with grilled meat, sausage, chicken and fish.

5 VINE-RIPENED TOMATOES, SEEDED
  AND FINELY DICED

2 GREEN CAPSICUMS (PEPPERS), SEEDED
  AND FINELY DICED

1 WHITE ONION, FINELY DICED

2 TABLESPOONS CHOPPED FLAT-LEAF
  (ITALIAN) PARSLEY

2 TABLESPOONS CHOPPED CORIANDER
  (CILANTRO) LEAVES

¾ CUP (185 ML/6½ FL OZ) EXTRA-VIRGIN
  OLIVE OIL

¾ CUP (185 ML/6½ FL OZ) WHITE VINEGAR

Combine the tomato, capsicum, onion, parsley and coriander in a medium-sized bowl. Add the olive oil and vinegar and stir well to combine.

Any leftover salsa can be stored in an airtight container in the refrigerator for up to 2 days.

MAKES 5 CUPS

FAMILY GATHERINGS

SERVES 10–12

GRILLED CORNBREAD STUFFED WITH CHEESE 32

GUASACACA (AVOCADO SAUCE) 114

MARINATED ROAST PORK LEG 94

STEAMED FRESH CORN PARCELS 123

SALT-BAKED POTATOES (USE 12 POTATOES) 128

PALM HEART SALAD 126

BRAZILIAN COCONUT BAKED CUSTARD CAKE 185

1½ × PORTIONS CLERICO 199

2 DAYS BEFORE:

- Marinate Pork Leg in spice mix and lime juice

THE DAY BEFORE:

- Marinate Pork Leg in beer
- Make Brazilian Coconut Baked Custard Cake

MORNING OF:

- Prepare and shape Cornbreads Stuffed with Cheese, cover and refrigerate
- Prepare *Guasacaca* (Avocado Sauce), cover and refrigerate
- Prepare Fresh Corn Parcels, cover and refrigerate
- Prepare and wrap Salt-baked Potatoes, set aside

2 HOURS BEFORE GUESTS ARRIVE:

- Prepare *Clerico*, cover and refrigerate

1 HOUR BEFORE GUESTS ARRIVE:

- Preheat the barbecue
- Start grilling Pork Leg on the barbecue
- Prepare Palm Heart Salad, but do not dress

UPON GUESTS' ARRIVAL:

- Serve *Clerico*
- Grill and serve Grilled Cornbread Stuffed with Cheese and the *Guasacaca* (Avocado Sauce)
- Put Salt-baked Potatoes on to cook 30 minutes before pork leg is ready
- Check pork leg and once cooked remove, cover and rest
- Steam Fresh Corn Parcels
- Dress Palm Heart Salad
- Slice Pork Leg and serve with Salt-baked Potatoes, Steamed Fresh Corn Parcels, Palm Heart Salad and any remaining *Guasacaca* (Avocado Sauce)
- Serve Brazilian Coconut Baked Custard Cake when ready

SIDES

FAROFA

BRAZILIAN TOASTED MANIOC FLOUR WITH EGG, BACON AND ONION

Farofa is toasted manioc (cassava) flour which is made from ground cassava root. The flour is gluten-free and has a coarse texture similar to a fine couscous or breadcrumbs. It is a unique side dish originating from the Brazilian native Indians. It is commonly served with grilled meats at barbecues and as part of the national dish *feijoada*, a pork and black bean stew. It can also be used as a stuffing for poultry and fish. There are many variations to the dish — sometimes banana and nuts can be added, or try dried fruits, such as raisins.

80 G (3 OZ) BUTTER

I LARGE ONION, THINLY SLICED

2 GARLIC CLOVES, FINELY CHOPPED

250 G (9 OZ) BACON, FINELY CHOPPED

4 LARGE EGGS, LIGHTLY BEATEN

500 G (I LB 2 OZ) MANIOC (CASSAVA) FLOUR

Melt the butter in a saucepan over low–medium heat. Add the onion and garlic and cook until softened. Add the bacon and cook for 4–5 minutes, or until golden brown. Add the egg and cook, stirring constantly, until the egg has scrambled.

Add the manioc flour to the pan and continue to cook for a further 10 minutes, stirring occasionally, until golden brown — the mixture will be quite dry. Season the *farofa* with sea salt and freshly ground black pepper, to taste. Serve warm or at room temperature with grilled meat, chicken or fish.

NOTE: Manioc flour can be purchased from Latin American food stores or online.

SERVES 8–10

ARROZ BRANCO

BRAZILIAN RICE

Rice is a staple dish in many countries and it is eaten almost daily as a side dish in Brazil. It was introduced to Brazil by Portuguese African slaves. Rice in Brazil is cooked using the absorption method, where the exact amount of water required is used to cook the rice, leaving you with light, fluffy and separated grains. It is served to accompany bean dishes such as Black Bean Stew (page 135) and alongside barbecued meats, poultry and fish.

2 CUPS (400 G/14 OZ) BASMATI RICE

2 TABLESPOONS OLIVE OIL

2 GARLIC CLOVES, CRUSHED

1 TEASPOON SEA SALT

Place the rice in a fine mesh sieve and rinse under cold running water, until the water runs clear. Drain well.

Heat the olive oil in a heavy-based saucepan over low–medium heat. Add the garlic and cook until softened. Add the rice and cook, stirring constantly, for 1–2 minutes, or until lightly toasted.

Add 3 cups (750 ml/25 fl oz) water to the rice in the pan and season with the salt. Bring to the boil, then reduce the heat to low, cover, and cook for 12 minutes, or until the rice is tender and all of the water has been absorbed. Remove from the heat, leave the lid on the pan, and set aside to finish cooking for a further 5 minutes.

Fluff the rice with a fork and transfer to a serving dish. Serve hot.

SERVES 6–8

HUMITAS

STEAMED FRESH CORN PARCELS

Humitas are similar to Mexican *tamales*, however these corn parcels are filled with a freshly ground corn mixture instead of dried ground corn. Common throughout South America, *humitas* vary from region to region and even house to house.

8 COBS SWEET CORN WITH HUSK ON

40 G (1½ OZ) BUTTER

1 ONION, FINELY CHOPPED

½ CUP (125 ML/4 FL OZ) FULL-CREAM
  (WHOLE) MILK

150 G (5 OZ) QUESO FRESCO CHEESE,
  COARSELY GRATED (SEE NOTE)

½ TEASPOON DRIED CHILLI FLAKES

Peel back and remove the corn husks, taking care not to tear them as they will later be used to wrap the corn parcels. Remove and discard the silk. Coarsely grate the corn into a bowl and set aside.

Melt the butter in a saucepan over low–medium heat. Add the onion and cook until softened. Add the corn and its juice and cook for 3–5 minutes, or until the liquid reduces and the mixture begins to thicken. Pour in the milk and bring to the boil. Reduce the heat and simmer gently for 5–10 minutes, stirring occasionally until the corn has softened and thickened. Remove from the heat, stir in half of the *queso fresco* and season with sea salt. Set aside.

Soak the corn husks in boiling water for 1–2 minutes, or until softened and pliable. Refresh under cold running water. Drain well.

To make the corn parcels, lay one large or two small corn husks (side by side) on a clean work surface. Lay another corn husk across the middle to make a cross. Place a large spoonful of the corn mixture into the centre. Sprinkle a little of the remaining *queso fresco* on the parcels and top with chilli flakes. Fold the sides of one of the husks over the filling and then fold the remaining husk over the top to make a square parcel. Tear a couple of corn husks into thin strips to use as ties and secure. Repeat with the remaining corn mixture and husks.

Place the *humitas* in a steamer and set over boiling water. Steam for 5–10 minutes, or until heated through. Serve hot or at room temperature with grilled meat, chicken or fish.

NOTE: Queso fresco, or 'fresh cheese', is a firm white South American cheese made from cow's milk or a combination of cow's and goat's milk. Substitute goat's cheese if unavailable.

MAKES 16

ENSALADA DE PALMITOS

PALM HEART SALAD

Palm hearts are the tender inner core of the growing bud of the palm tree. They have a velvety texture and subtle flavour similar to artichokes. They are popular in Brazilian cuisine and are often served simply dressed with olive oil as an appetiser, in salads or as a filling for empanadas. They can be purchased from Latin American food stores, usually in glass jars or tins.

1 x 400 G (14 OZ) TIN PALM HEARTS, DRAINED
   AND CUT INTO 1.5 CM (½ INCH) THICK
   ROUNDS
4 VINE-RIPENED TOMATOES, SLICED INTO
   1 CM (½ INCH) ROUNDS
½ RED ONION, THINLY SLICED
100 G (3½ OZ) BABY SPINACH LEAVES
2 TEASPOONS DIJON MUSTARD
JUICE OF 2 LIMES
1 CUP (80 ML/3 FL OZ) EXTRA-VIRGIN
   OLIVE OIL

Combine the palm hearts, tomato, onion and spinach leaves in a medium-sized serving bowl.

To make the dressing, whisk together the mustard and lime juice in a small bowl. Gradually pour in the olive oil in a thin steady stream, whisking to combine; season with sea salt and freshly ground black pepper, to taste.

Pour the dressing over the salad and toss to combine. Serve with grilled meat, chicken or fish.

SERVES 6

PAPAS ASADAS A LA SAL

SALT-BAKED POTATOES

These potatoes have a crisp and golden skin, while the salt crust ensures they are moist and fluffy on the inside. They are infused with a subtle salt flavour, without becoming overly salty and are delicious as they are, requiring no extra seasoning or butter. They are easy to throw onto a barbecue while meat dishes are cooking and they make a very versatile accompaniment to just about any grill.

3 KG (6 LB 9 OZ) TABLE SALT

8 ROASTING POTATOES, SUCH AS NICOLA,
   WASHED

EXTRA-VIRGIN OLIVE OIL, FOR DRIZZLING
   (OPTIONAL)

Preheat a gas or charcoal barbecue chargrill or hotplate to medium.

Put the salt into a kitchen sink and add 1½ cups (375 ml/12½ fl oz) water. Use your hands to mix together the salt compact, adding a little more water if required.

Cut eight pieces of foil, large enough to individually wrap each potato. Divide half of the salt mixture evenly between the foil pieces. Place the potatoes on top and cover with the remaining salt. Wrap up securely, ensuring each potato is completely encased in salt and sealed in foil.

Place the parcels on the grill or hotplate, or bury in hot coals and cook, turning occasionally, for 45–60 minutes, or until the potatoes are crisp on the outside and tender on the inside. Insert a skewer through the foil and salt layer to test.

To serve, unwrap the foil and crack the salt using the back of a spoon. Remove the potatoes from the salt, dusting off any excess, then drizzle with olive oil, if desired.

SERVES 8

CEBOLLAS COCIDAS AL HORNO CON ROMERO

BAKED ROSEMARY ONIONS

These onions make a simple side dish using only three ingredients. But don't be fooled — when combined and baked on the barbecue the onions soften and the sugars caramelise making them sticky sweet, while the aromatic rosemary is infused, blending a delightful combination of flavours.

8 RED ONIONS

3 SPRIGS ROSEMARY

EXTRA-VIRGIN OLIVE OIL, FOR DRIZZLING
(OPTIONAL)

Preheat a gas or charcoal barbecue chargrill or hotplate to medium.

Cut eight pieces of foil that are large enough to individually wrap each onion.

Peel the onions and cut each onion through the centre into quarters, keeping the bases intact. Use your fingers to open the onions slightly, stuff with a little rosemary and season with sea salt and freshly ground black pepper.

Put each onion on a piece of foil and drizzle with oil. Wrap to seal and enclose the onions.

Place the parcels on the grill or hotplate or bury in hot coals. Cook for 30–40 minutes, turning occasionally, until tender. Insert a skewer through the foil to test.

To serve, unwrap the foil and transfer to a serving plate. Drizzle with olive oil, if desired. Serve with grilled meat, chicken or fish.

SERVES 8

HALLAQUITAS

VENEZUELAN CORN PARCELS

Hallaquitas are the Venezuelan version of the Mexican *tamales*. They are boiled corn parcels filled with a dough made from dried corn, which is wrapped in dried corn husks. *Hallaquitas* are tied twice, once at the top and then in the middle, creating a kind of waist. Curvaceous women in Venezuela are referred to as *hallaquitas* as their curves resemble the corn parcels. Dried corn husks are available from Latin American food stores.

40 G (1½ OZ) BUTTER

3 TEASPOONS SEA SALT

30 DRIED CORN HUSKS

3 CUPS (550 G/1 LB 4 OZ) MASAREPA (SEE NOTE)

¾ CUP (90 G/3¼ OZ) GRATED PARMESAN CHEESE

½ RED CAPSICUM (PEPPER), SEEDED AND VERY
    FINELY CHOPPED

Put the butter, salt and 3½ cups (870 ml/29 fl oz) water in a medium-sized saucepan over low heat and stir until the butter has melted and the salt has dissolved. Remove from the heat and set aside for 10 minutes, to cool slightly.

Meanwhile, place the corn husks in a medium-sized bowl, cover with hot water and set aside for 15 minutes, to soak. Drain and set aside.

Gradually pour the masarepa into the cooled water, stirring to form a dough. Turn the dough out onto a clean work surface, add the cheese and capsicum and knead to incorporate. Add a little extra masarepa if the dough is too wet, or a drizzle of water if it is too dry.

Divide the dough into 24 equal-sized portions. Shape each portion in an oval-shaped ball.

Place a ball of corn dough lengthwise in the centre of a pre-soaked corn husk. Fold up the bottom of the husk and fold in the sides to encase the corn filling. Tear a couple of corn husks into thin strips to use as ties. Tie each parcel twice, once at the top and then in the middle, to create a kind of waist. Repeat with the remaining filling and husks to make 24 parcels in total.

Bring a large saucepan of salted water to the boil. Cook the *hallaquitas* for 10–15 minutes, or until firm. Unwrap the husks to eat.

NOTE: Masarepa is a pre-cooked ground corn flour. It can be sourced from Latin American food stores. It is also called masa harina.

MAKES 24

MENESTRA

LENTIL STEW

Menestra is a thick vegetarian stew from Ecuador. It is typically made from lentils, however beans or chickpeas can also be used. It is hearty and warming and makes a wonderful addition to a winter barbecue. It is traditionally served with grilled meats, rice and Twice-fried Plantain Chips (page 152).

2 TABLESPOONS VEGETABLE OIL

I RED ONION, FINELY DICED

3 GARLIC CLOVES, FINELY DICED

I TEASPOON GROUND CUMIN

2 VINE-RIPENED TOMATOES, PEELED, SEEDED
    AND DICED

I SMALL GREEN CAPSICUM (PEPPER),
    SEEDED AND FINELY DICED

2 CUPS (430 G/15¼ OZ) BROWN LENTILS,
    RINSED

I SMALL HANDFUL CORIANDER (CILANTRO)
    LEAVES, CHOPPED

Heat the vegetable oil in a large heavy-based saucepan over low–medium heat. Add the onion and garlic and cook until softened. Add the cumin and cook until fragrant. Add the tomato and capsicum and cook for 3–4 minutes, or until softened.

Add the lentils and 4 cups (I litre/34 fl oz) water to the pan and bring to the boil. Reduce the heat to low and simmer for 20 minutes, or until the lentils are tender and the water has reduced to make a thick stew. Season with sea salt and freshly ground black pepper.

Transfer the stew to a serving bowl and sprinkle with the coriander. Serve hot.

SERVES 8

FEIJÃO

BLACK BEAN STEW

This hearty black bean stew is commonplace in Brazil. It can be made a day in advance, allowing time for the smoky bacon flavour to infuse. Alternatively, if preparing on the day, to save time you can cook the beans in a pressure cooker for only 25 minutes instead of 1½ hours. Proceed with the remainder of the recipe as instructed.

500 G (1 LB 2 OZ) DRIED BLACK BEANS, SOAKED
    IN COLD WATER OVERNIGHT
2 BAY LEAVES
2 TABLESPOONS OLIVE OIL
1 ONION, FINELY CHOPPED
3 GARLIC CLOVES, FINELY CHOPPED
2 SLICES BACON, ROUGHLY CHOPPED

Drain the beans and place in a large heavy-based saucepan. Add 6 cups (1.5 litres/51 fl oz) water and the bay leaves and bring to the boil. Reduce the heat to low and simmer for 1–1½ hours, or until the beans are just tender. This may take longer, depending on the age of your beans. Remove from the heat and set aside. Do not drain.

Heat the oil in a saucepan over low–medium heat. Add the onion and garlic and cook until softened. Add the bacon and cook for 3–5 minutes, or until browned. Pour in the beans and their cooking liquid and stir to combine. Simmer for a further 15 minutes, or until the liquid reduces and the mixture thickens; season with sea salt and freshly ground black pepper.

Transfer to a large serving bowl and serve hot with Brazilian Rice (page 122). This stew is a good accompaniment to any grilled meats.

SERVES 8

PIMIENTOS ROJOS ASADOS

GRILLED RED CAPSICUM

Blackening the capsicum's (pepper's) skins not only makes it easy for them to be removed but also imparts a subtle smoky flavour. When peeled, the stunning bright red flesh is revealed — it is tender and sweet and requires little more than some olive oil, garlic and herbs for contrasting colour.

5 LARGE RED CAPSICUMS (PEPPERS)

½ CUP (125 ML/4 FL OZ) OLIVE OIL

1 SMALL HANDFUL FLAT-LEAF (ITALIAN) PARSLEY, CHOPPED

5 GARLIC CLOVES, THINLY SLICED

Preheat a gas or charcoal barbecue to medium–high.

Place the capsicums on the grill or directly into the hot coals and cook for 10–15 minutes, turning occasionally, until all sides are blackened and blistered. Remove from the heat and place into a large bowl. Cover with plastic wrap and set aside for 15 minutes — this will make it easier to remove the skins.

Peel and discard the skins, cut each capsicum in half lengthwise and remove and discard the seeds. Slice the flesh into thick strips and place in a serving dish. Pour over the olive oil and stir through the parsley and garlic slices; season with sea salt and freshly ground black pepper.

SERVES 8

ENSALADA DE QUINOA

QUINOA SALAD

Quinoa, pronounced '*keen-wah*', is a seed originating from the Andes mountains in Peru. It is high in protein, amino acids and magnesium and has been labelled a 'super food' in the West. Its high protein value makes it an excellent choice for vegetarians. It is quick and easy to prepare and is highly versatile.

I CUP (200 G/7 OZ) QUINOA

2 LEBANESE (SHORT) CUCUMBERS

250 G (9 OZ) CHERRY TOMATOES

5 SPRING ONIONS (SCALLIONS)

2 LONG GREEN CHILLIES, SEEDED AND
   FINELY CHOPPED

I GRAPEFRUIT

I HANDFUL FLAT-LEAF (ITALIAN) PARSLEY,
   CHOPPED

I LARGE HANDFUL MINT LEAVES, CHOPPED

2 TABLESPOONS LIME JUICE

¼ CUP (60 ML/2 FL OZ) OLIVE OIL

Put the quinoa and 2 cups (500 ml/17 fl oz) water in a large saucepan over medium–high heat and bring to the boil. Reduce the heat to low, cover, and simmer for 12–15 minutes, or until the liquid has been absorbed and the quinoa is light and fluffy. Spread out on a tray and set aside to cool.

Dice the cucumbers, quarter the cherry tomatoes and thinly slice the spring onions and place into a large bowl.

Slice the ends off the grapefruit and cut away the skin and pith. Hold the grapefruit over the bowl of vegetables and cut away the segments letting the juice and segments fall into the bowl.

Add the cooled quinoa, parsley and mint to the vegetables. Pour in the lime juice and olive oil and stir to combine. Season with sea salt and freshly ground black pepper, to taste, before serving.

SERVES 6—8

PLÁTANOS A LA PLANCHA COM MIGAS DE PAN

GRILLED PLANTAIN IN BREADCRUMBS

Plantains are typically used for cooking savoury dishes. They are eaten in parts of South America, Africa and Southeast Asia. They are cooked in similar ways to potatoes and can be steamed, boiled or fried. Here they are coated in breadcrumbs, but they are commonly fried without them. They are traditionally served to accompany grilled meats.

5 LARGE GREEN PLANTAIN BANANAS

4 LARGE EGGS

2 CUPS (220 G/8 OZ) DRIED BREADCRUMBS

60 G (2 OZ) BUTTER

2 TABLESPOONS VEGETABLE OIL

Preheat a gas barbecue grill plate to medium.

Cut the plantain bananas in half lengthwise.

Lightly beat the eggs in a large shallow bowl. Place the breadcrumbs on a tray.

Dip the plantain halves first into the egg and then roll to coat in the breadcrumbs, pressing to coat all over.

Heat the butter and vegetable oil together in a small saucepan, until the butter has melted.

Grease the grill plate with half of the butter mixture. Cook the plantain for 3–5 minutes on one side, drizzle with the remaining butter mixture, then turn and cook the other side for a further 3–5 minutes, or until golden brown and soft.

SERVES 10

MAIZ A LA PARRILLA TRES FORMAS

GRILLED CORN THREE WAYS

Grilled corn South American–style looks and tastes fabulous. You can serve it simply on its own, or choose one of the toppings below for an additional burst of flavour — these are quick and easy to prepare and are sprinkled or smeared over the hot corn cobs when they come off the grill — delicious!

8 COBS SWEET CORN WITH HUSKS ON

80 G (3 OZ) BUTTER, AT ROOM TEMPERATURE

SPICED TOPPING

2 TEASPOONS SMOKED PAPRIKA

1 TEASPOON GROUND CUMIN

1 TEASPOON SEA SALT

CHILLI AND LIME BUTTER

120 G (4 OZ) BUTTER, SOFTENED

½ TEASPOON DRIED CHILLI FLAKES

FINELY GRATED ZEST OF 1 LIME

CHEESE TOPPING

120 G (4 OZ) QUESO FRESCO CHEESE,
    FINELY GRATED (SEE NOTE PAGE 123)

To grill the corn, peel back the corn husks, leaving them attached at the base, then remove and discard the stringy silk.

Wrap the corn cobs back into the husks and soak in cold water for 15 minutes. This helps to prevent the husks from catching fire. Drain and squeeze out any excess water.

Peel back the husks, smear the corn with butter and season with sea salt. Re-cover in the husks.

Preheat a charcoal or gas barbecue grill to medium–high. Cook the corn for 10–15 minutes, turning occasionally, until the corn cobs are beginning to char slightly. At this stage you can make any of the following flavourings if you wish.

To make the spiced flavouring, combine all of the spiced topping ingredients in a bowl.

To make the chilli and lime butter, combine all of the ingredients in a bowl.

Peel back the husks and grill the cobs for a further 10 minutes, turning occasionally, until lightly charred. Serve the corn cobs hot on their own or sprinkle with the cheese or smear your preferred flavourings over the hot cobs before serving.

SERVES 8

ENSALADA DE PALLARES

LIMA BEAN SALAD

This colourful salad is made using the native bean of Peru, the lima bean, which takes its name from the country's capital city. With the addition of tomatoes, onion, herbs and the South American cheese *queso fresco*, a firm mild-tasting, yet slightly salty cheese, this salad makes a satisfying side dish for meat eaters and vegetarians alike.

400 G (14 OZ/2 CUPS) DRIED LIMA BEANS,
    SOAKED IN COLD WATER OVERNIGHT

1 RED ONION, THINLY SLICED

3 LARGE TOMATOES, DICED

200 G (7 OZ) QUESO FRESCO, CRUMBLED
    (SEE NOTE PAGE 123)

1 LARGE HANDFUL FLAT-LEAF
    (ITALIAN) PARSLEY, CHOPPED

JUICE OF 1 LIME

1 TABLESPOON RED WINE VINEGAR

½ TEASPOON CASTER (SUPERFINE) SUGAR

¼ CUP (60 ML/2 FL OZ) EXTRA-VIRGIN
    OLIVE OIL

Drain the lima beans and place them in a large saucepan, cover with about 8 cups (2 litres/68 fl oz) water and bring to the boil over high heat. Reduce the heat to low and simmer for 20–30 minutes, or until the beans are just tender. Rinse immediately under cold water to stop the cooking process, then drain well and set aside to cool.

Combine the beans, onion, tomato, *queso fresco* and parsley in a medium-sized serving bowl.

Combine the lime juice, vinegar and sugar in a small bowl. Gradually whisk in the olive oil and season with sea salt and freshly ground black pepper. Pour over the salad and toss to combine.

SERVES 6

CHICORY CON TOMATES A LA PLANCHA

GRILLED WITLOF AND TOMATO

This simple grilled tomato and witlof side dish can be easily prepared and cooked while your meat is resting. Tomatoes are delicious grilled, their sugars caramelising as they begin to char, while witlof's characteristic bitterness is mellowed when its crisp leaves soften on the grill. Drizzled with olive oil and lemon juice and accompanied by smoky grilled lemon halves this dish makes a quick and easy yet interesting addition to grilled meats, chicken and fish.

8 VINE-RIPENED TOMATOES, HALVED
    CROSSWISE

4 WITLOF (CHICORY/BELGIAN ENDIVE),
    HALVED LENGTHWISE

½ CUP (125 ML/4 FL OZ) OLIVE OIL

VEGETABLE OIL, FOR BRUSHING

I LEMON, HALVED

¼ CUP (60 ML/2 FL OZ) LEMON JUICE

Preheat a gas or charcoal barbecue chargrill to medium–high.

Place the tomatoes and witlof on a large tray, season with sea salt and freshly ground black pepper and drizzle with half of the olive oil.

Brush a little vegetable oil over the grill and cook the witlof for 4–5 minutes on each side, or until lightly charred. Grill the tomatoes and lemon halves, cut side down, for 3–4 minutes, or until lightly charred.

Arrange the witlof and tomato on a platter and drizzle with the remaining olive oil and the lemon juice. Serve with the grilled lemon halves, for squeezing over.

SERVES 8

GRILLED WITLOF AND TOMATO

SALADA DE BATATAS

BRAZILIAN POTATO SALAD

Potato salad is a standard side dish at most barbecues in South America. Here is the Brazilian version made with carrots, egg and olives. A good-quality mayonnaise is a must to avoid the dish becoming too sweet. There are variations of this salad throughout South America, the most common known as *Ensalada Rusa*, or Russian salad, which contains a mixture of vegetables.

1.5 KG (3 LB 5 OZ) POTATOES, PEELED AND
 CUT INTO 2.5 CM (1 INCH) CUBES

5 CARROTS, PEELED AND CUT INTO 2 CM
 (¾ INCH) CUBES

4 LARGE HARD-BOILED EGGS, PEELED AND
 ROUGHLY CHOPPED

½ CUP (90 G/3¼ OZ) PITTED GREEN OLIVES

½ CUP (125 G/4 OZ) GOOD-QUALITY
 WHOLE-EGG MAYONNAISE

Place the potatoes and carrots in separate saucepans. Cover with cold water and season with salt. Cook over medium heat for 10–15 minutes, or until just tender. Drain and set aside to cool.

Combine the potato, carrot, egg and olives in a medium-sized bowl. Add the mayonnaise and stir to combine. Before serving, season with sea salt and freshly ground black pepper, to taste.

Serve the Brazilian potato salad with grilled meat, chicken or fish.

SERVES 8

PATACONES

TWICE-FRIED PLANTAIN CHIPS

Patacones are made by twice-frying rounds of unripe plantain. When cooked, plantain tastes similar to potato and when fried they have a lovely crunchy texture. *Patacones* are eaten in Ecuador, Colombia and Peru as well as Venezuela, where they are known as *tostones*. They can be eaten as a starter, seasoned simply with sea salt or can be served as a side to accompany grilled meats.

4 LARGE GREEN PLANTAIN BANANAS

VEGETABLE OIL, FOR FRYING

Peel the plantains using a small sharp knife and cut into 2.5 cm (1 inch) thick rounds.

Pour enough vegetable oil into a large frying pan to come approximately 1.5 cm (½ inch) up the side of the pan. Heat the oil over medium–high heat and fry the plantain, in batches, for 2 minutes on each side, or until light golden. Remove from the oil using a slotted spoon and drain on paper towels.

Place a few plantain rounds between two pieces of baking paper and press down to squash the rounds, using the base of a small saucepan or the palm of your hand (if they're not too hot), to make flat discs.

Reheat the oil over medium–high heat and re-fry the plantain discs, in batches, for 1–2 minutes, or until golden brown. Drain on paper towels. Season the plantain chips with sea salt and serve hot with grilled meats or on their own as a snack.

SERVES 8–12

BERENJENAS CON AJI Y OREGANO LA PARRILLA

GRILLED EGGPLANT WITH CHILLI AND OREGANO

Eggplants require salting before grilling to draw out any bitterness from the flesh. When cooked on the barbecue, the outside of the eggplant becomes slightly charred while the flesh becomes soft and creamy and gives the eggplant a slightly smoky flavour. The addition of oregano, salt and chilli for seasoning melds perfectly to make this side an ideal accompaniment to grilled meats.

2 EGGPLANTS (AUBERGINES)

1 CUP (80 ML/3 FL OZ) OLIVE OIL

1 GARLIC CLOVE, CRUSHED

1 TABLESPOON SEA SALT

1 TABLESPOON DRIED OREGANO

2 TEASPOONS DRIED CHILLI FLAKES, CRUSHED

Trim the ends off the eggplants and cut into 1.5 cm (½ inch) thick rounds. Place on a wire rack, sprinkle generously with salt and set aside for 30 minutes. Rinse off the salt under cold running water and pat dry using paper towels.

Combine the olive oil and garlic in a small bowl. Combine the salt, oregano and chilli flakes in a separate small bowl.

Preheat a gas or charcoal barbecue chargrill to medium.

Drizzle the eggplant rounds with the garlic oil and sprinkle both sides with the herb and spice mix. Grill the eggplant for 3 minutes on each side, or until softened and lightly charred. Transfer to a serving bowl and serve hot.

SERVES 8

PAN CON AJO Y ROMERO A LA PARRILLA

ARGENTINIAN GRILLED GARLIC AND ROSEMARY FLAT BREAD

No South American barbecue is complete without bread. These flatbreads have the consistency of pizza dough. They are extremely easy to make and the garlic and rosemary oil infuses a wonderful flavour when the dough is grilled.

FLAT BREAD

3½ CUPS (525 G/1 LB 2¾ OZ) PLAIN
    (ALL-PURPOSE) FLOUR
2 TEASPOONS SEA SALT
2 TEASPOONS (7 G/¼ OZ) ACTIVE DRIED YEAST
1 TABLESPOON OLIVE OIL

GARLIC AND ROSEMARY OIL

2 GARLIC CLOVES, FINELY CHOPPED
¼ CUP (60 ML/2 FL OZ) EXTRA-VIRGIN
    OLIVE OIL
2 TEASPOONS SEA SALT
1 SMALL HANDFUL ROSEMARY LEAVES

To make the flat bread, put the flour, salt, yeast, oil and 1⅓ cups (330 ml/11 fl oz) warm water into an electric mixer fitted with a dough hook attachment. Mix on low–medium speed for 5 minutes, or until the mixture comes together to form a smooth elastic dough. Alternatively, knead the dough by hand for 10–15 minutes. Transfer to a lightly oiled bowl, cover with a clean tea towel and set in a warm place to prove for 1–1½ hours, or until doubled in size.

Knock back the dough, using your fists to punch out all the air. Shape into four even-sized balls and flatten slightly. Place on lightly oiled baking trays, cover with a clean tea towel and set in a warm place to prove for a further 30 minutes, or until doubled in size.

Preheat a gas or charcoal barbecue to medium–high. To make the garlic and rosemary oil, put all of the ingredients in a bowl and stir well to combine.

Flatten the dough out to 1 cm (½ inch) thick discs. Brush the top of each disc with the garlic and rosemary oil and grill, oil side down, for 5 minutes, or until golden brown. Brush the remaining side with oil, turn and cook for a further 5 minutes, or until cooked through. Cut into wedges and serve the flat bread hot or cold.

SERVES 8

BRAZILIAN CHURRASCO

SERVES 8–10

GRILLED BRAZILIAN GARLIC BREAD 20
GRILLED CHICKEN HEARTS 24
PICANHA (RUMP CAP) 44–45
LINGUICA SAUSAGES (SEE SOUTH AMERICAN SAUSAGES) 100
BRAZILIAN POTATO SALAD 148
FAROFA 120
VINAGRETE (BRAZILIAN SALSA) 115
BRAZILIAN CRÈME CARAMEL 166
CAIPIRINHAS 193

DAY BEFORE:

- Prepare Brazilian Crème Caramel and refrigerate
- Prepare Brazilian Garlic Bread sauce, cover and refrigerate

DAY OF:

- Make Vinagrete, cover and refrigerate
- Prepare Brazilian Potato Salad, cover and refrigerate

4 HOURS BEFORE GUESTS ARRIVE:

- Marinate Chicken Hearts

1 HOUR BEFORE GUESTS ARRIVE:

- Slice Picanha into steaks, then thread onto skewers
- Thread Chicken Hearts onto skewers
- Prepare Farofa
- Set up bar for making Caipirinhas

UPON GUESTS' ARRIVAL:

- Preheat the barbecue
- Make a large jug of Caipirinha and serve
- Cook and serve Brazilian Garlic Bread
- Cook and serve Chicken Hearts
- Cook Linguica Sausages, slice and serve
- Put Picanha on the barbecue to cook
- Slice and serve Picanha with Brazilian Potato Salad, Farofa and Vinagrete
- Serve Brazilian Crème Caramel when ready

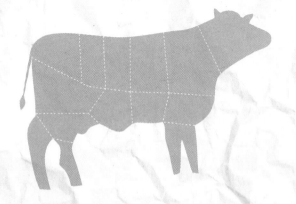

PAPA A LA HUANCAINA

PERUVIAN POTATOES WITH SPICY YELLOW CHEESE SAUCE

Papa a la Huancaina is a Peruvian-style potato salad originating from and named after the city Huancayo. It is traditionally made using boiled potatoes but here the potatoes are baked in parcels on the barbecue until crisp and golden brown. Topped with a thick and creamy cheese sauce made bright yellow and spiced with the Peruvian chilli, *aji amarillo*, it has a lovely lingering warmth.

CHEESE SAUCE

2 TABLESPOONS VEGETABLE OIL

½ BROWN ONION, CHOPPED

2 GARLIC CLOVES, CHOPPED

2–3 TABLESPOONS AJI AMARILLO PASTE (SEE NOTE)

150 G (5 OZ) QUESO FRESCO, ROUGHLY CHOPPED (SEE NOTE PAGE 123)

1 CUP (80 ML/3 FL OZ) EVAPORATED MILK

1 KG (2 LB 3 OZ) RED OR PURPLE POTATOES, CUT INTO 2.5 CM (1 INCH) CUBES

OLIVE OIL, FOR DRIZZLING

2 HARD-BOILED EGGS, PEELED AND QUARTERED, TO SERVE

¼ CUP (30 G/1 OZ) BLACK PITTED OLIVES, TO SERVE

To make the yellow cheese sauce, heat the vegetable oil in a medium-sized frying pan over low–medium heat. Add the onion and garlic and cook until softened. Add the *aji amarillo* paste and cook until fragrant. Remove from the heat, allow to cool slightly, then transfer to a food processor and process until smooth. Add the *queso fresco* and continue to process to make a coarse paste. Gradually pour in the evaporated milk and ¼ cup (60 ml/2 fl oz) water and process to make a smooth thick sauce. Transfer to a small bowl and set aside.

Preheat a gas or charcoal barbecue to medium.

Cut two pieces of foil, large enough to wrap the potato in two batches. Divide the potato among the foil pieces and drizzle with olive oil. Wrap to seal and enclose the potato.

Place the parcels on the grill plate or bury in hot coals and cook for 30–45 minutes, turning occasionally, until the potatoes are tender. Insert a skewer through the foil and into the potatoes to test if they are done.

To serve, unwrap the potato parcels and transfer to a large serving bowl. Drizzle with the prepared sauce and scatter with the boiled egg and olives. Serve hot with grilled meat, chicken or fish.

NOTE: Amarillo chillies are Peruvian hot yellow chillies. Aji amarillo paste can be sourced from Latin American food stores. Alternatively, seed and soak dried amarillo chillies in just enough boiling water to cover, then drain and blend to a purée. You can substitute ½ yellow capsicum (pepper), 1 bird's eye chilli and 1 teaspoon ground turmeric for the aji amarillo paste, if necessary.

SERVES 8

♥ DESSERTS

PUDIM DE LEITE

BRAZILIAN CRÈME CARAMEL

This crème caramel is made using condensed milk, which South Americans are guilty of using to create super-sweet desserts. It can be made the day before you wish to serve it, making it an easy option for entertaining.

1 CUP (220 G/8 OZ) SUGAR

4 LARGE EGGS

2 x 395 G (13¾ OZ) TINS CONDENSED MILK

3¼ CUPS (810 ML/27 FL OZ) FULL-CREAM
(WHOLE) MILK

Preheat the oven to 180°C (350°F).

To make the caramel, combine the sugar and ½ cup (125 ml/4 fl oz) water together in a small saucepan over medium heat. Bring to the boil, then reduce the heat to low–medium and simmer, brushing down the sides of the pan occasionally with cold water to prevent the sugar from crystallising, until the liquid turns a golden brown caramel colour. Pour into the base of a 22 cm (8½ inch) ring tin and swirl to coat the base. Set aside for 10 minutes to harden.

Meanwhile, to make the custard, lightly beat the eggs in a medium-sized bowl. Add the condensed milk and full-cream milk and stir to combine. Pour into the tin.

Place the tin in a deep baking tray and pour enough hot water into the tray to come halfway up the side of the tin. Bake in the oven for 1½ hours, or until the custard has set — it should be just firm to the touch.

Remove the tray from the oven. Carefully remove the tin and set aside for 20 minutes to cool slightly, then refrigerate until completely cool.

To serve, run a knife around the edge of the crème caramel, dip the base of the tin into a bowl of hot water for 15 seconds and invert onto a serving plate.

SERVES 12

DULCE DE LECHE

ARGENTINIAN CARAMEL SAUCE

Dulce de leche translates as 'milk jam' or 'milk candy' and is a simple thick and rich caramel sauce that is made using a tin of condensed milk. It is a staple in every Argentinian kitchen and is commonly available pre-made in tins. It has a multitude of uses — it can be added as a filling to cakes, biscuits, crepes and doughnut-type desserts. It can also be served with ice cream or as a filling for *Alfajores* (page 172).

1 x 395 G (13¾ OZ) TIN CONDENSED MILK

To make the caramel sauce using a pressure cooker, place a trivet in the base of a pressure cooker. Set the tin of condensed milk on top and cover completely with water. Bring to high pressure over high heat and cook for 1 hour, adjusting the heat as needed to maintain the pressure. Remove from the heat and allow the pressure to release completely before opening. Carefully remove the tin using kitchen tongs and a tea towel and set aside to cool completely before opening — the result will be a thick golden brown caramel.

To make the caramel sauce using a saucepan, place the tin of condensed milk in a medium-sized saucepan. Cover completely with water and bring to the boil over high heat. Reduce the heat to low and simmer for 3 hours, topping up with boiling water as required, so the tin is always completely submerged. Remove from the heat and then carefully remove the tin from the hot water using kitchen tongs and a tea towel. Set aside and allow the tin to cool completely before opening.

Any leftovers can be stored in an airtight container in the refrigerator for up to 2 weeks, although it is unlikely to last this long — it's delicious!

MAKES 395 G (13¾ OZ)

ROTISSERIE ABACAXI COM AÇÚCAR E CANELA

ROTISSERIE PINEAPPLE WITH CINNAMON SUGAR

This is a unique dessert that can be prepared on the barbecue. It is also traditionally eaten between courses throughout a meal to break through the rich flavours of grilled meats.

I LARGE SWEET RIPE PINEAPPLE

¼ CUP (50 G/2 OZ) CASTER (SUPERFINE) SUGAR

I TABLESPOON GROUND CINNAMON

VANILLA ICE CREAM, TO SERVE (OPTIONAL)

Using a large sharp knife, trim the ends off the pineapple and remove the skin and eyes.

Preheat a gas barbecue fitted with a rotisserie to 200°C (400°F). Insert the rotisserie attachment lengthwise through the centre of the pineapple.

Combine the sugar and cinnamon in a small bowl. Sprinkle onto a large tray. Turn the pineapple in the sugar to coat evenly.

Secure the rotisserie according to the manufacturer's instructions. Turn off the burners directly underneath the pineapple, leaving the side burners on medium. Place a drip tray filled with 1 cm (½ inch) water underneath the pineapple. Cook the pineapple for 20–25 minutes, or until it is hot and the sugar has caramelised.

Wearing barbecue mitts, carefully remove the rotisserie rod. Cut the pineapple into slices and serve hot with ice cream, if desired.

NOTE: If you do not have a rotisserie barbecue you can cut the pineapple into 2 cm (¾ inch) thick rounds and grill (broil) over medium heat for 3 minutes on each side, or until hot and caramelised.

SERVES 10–12

ALFAJORES

ARGENTINIAN CARAMEL BISCUIT SANDWICHES

Alfajores are a popular treat throughout South America. There are countless variations, depending on region. Essentially they are made of two delicate buttery biscuits which are used to sandwich a filling, most commonly *Dulche de leche* or Argentinian Caramel Sauce (page 168). They are then rolled in coconut or nuts, dipped in white or dark chocolate, coated in meringue or dusted with icing (confectioners') sugar. *Alfajores* are also found triple-layered or filled with jam or chocolate nut spread.

1½ CUPS (200 G/7 OZ) CORNFLOUR (CORNSTARCH), PLUS EXTRA FOR ROLLING

1 CUP (150 G/5 OZ) PLAIN (ALL-PURPOSE) FLOUR

½ CUP (60 G/3 OZ) ICING (CONFECTIONERS') SUGAR, PLUS EXTRA FOR DUSTING

225 G (8 OZ) UNSALTED BUTTER, MELTED AND COOLED, PLUS EXTRA FOR GREASING

1 x QUANTITY DULCE DE LECHE (PAGE 168)

1 CUP (90 G/3¼ OZ) DESICCATED COCONUT, FOR ROLLING

Preheat the oven to 180°C (350°F). Lightly grease two baking trays with a little melted butter.

Sift the cornflour, flour and icing sugar together in a medium-sized bowl. Pour in the melted butter and stir to combine. Turn out onto a clean work surface and knead to form a soft dough.

Lightly dust the work surface with a little extra cornflour and use a rolling pin to roll the dough out to a thickness of 1 cm (½ inch). Use a 6 cm (2½ inch) round pastry cutter to cut out circular rounds — you should make about 24 in total.

Arrange the rounds on the prepared baking trays and bake in the oven for 10 minutes, or until they begin to turn golden brown on the edges. Remove from the oven and allow to cool on the trays for 10 minutes, before transferring to a wire rack to cool completely.

Spread a thick layer of *dulce de leche* on half of the biscuits. Place the remaining biscuits on top and press down gently to secure. Roll the edge of the biscuits in desiccated coconut to coat, then lightly dust the tops with icing sugar.

The biscuits can be stored in an airtight container in the refrigerator for up to 3 days.

MAKES 12

PAPAYA ALEGRE

CHILEAN SPIKED PAPAYA WITH CREAM

This simple yet effective dessert is made using Pisco, a sweet grape brandy that heralds from Peru, although there is also a Chilean version of the drink — both are available from large bottle shops. Papaya contains an enzyme called papain, which helps to break down the proteins in meats, making this a perfect dessert to aid your digestion after a meaty South American barbecue.

I LARGE PAPAYA

I CUP (80 ML/3 FL OZ) ORANGE JUICE

30 ML (I FL OZ) PISCO

I CUP (250 ML/8½ FL OZ) POURING
   (WHIPPING) CREAM

½ TABLESPOON ICING (CONFECTIONERS')
   SUGAR

Cut the papaya in half lengthwise and scoop out the seeds. Remove the skin and cut the flesh into 2 cm (¾ inch) cubes. Place in a medium–sized bowl.

Combine the orange juice and Pisco in a small bowl. Pour over the papaya and toss to coat. Cover and refrigerate for 30 minutes.

Using an electric mixer fitted with a whisk attachment, whip together the cream and sugar until soft peaks form.

Transfer the papaya to a serving bowl and top with whipped cream, to serve.

SERVES 4

MOUSSE DE MARACUJA

BRAZILIAN PASSIONFRUIT MOUSSE

Passionfruit is the fruit of the native vine found growing in the rainforests of Brazil. In this dessert, the sweet tangy pulp is used to make a smooth and creamy mousse that has been sweetened with condensed milk. It is best to use fresh passionfruit, however if unavailable, you can substitute with tinned passionfruit pulp and adjust the sweetness by adding less condensed milk and more cream. This mousse can be made a day in advance and frozen.

I CUP (250 ML/8½ FL OZ) POURING (WHIPPING) CREAM

½ CUP (125 ML/4 FL OZ) TINNED CONDENSED MILK

½ CUP (125 ML/4 FL OZ) PASSIONFRUIT JUICE (STRAIN THE FRESH PULP OF ABOUT 8 PASSIONFRUIT), PLUS EXTRA PULP FOR DECORATING

I TABLESPOON LIME JUICE

Using an electric mixer fitted with a whisk attachment, whip the cream until soft peaks form.

In a separate bowl, mix together the condensed milk, passionfruit juice and lime juice. Add the cream and stir to combine. Pour into a 20 cm (8 inch) glass pie dish or six shallow serving glasses. Cover and refrigerate for I hour.

Drizzle with the extra passionfruit pulp, to serve.

SERVES 6

BRIGADERIOS

BRAZILIAN CHOCOLATE FUDGE TRUFFLES

Traditionally served at children's parties, these chewy little fudge balls make a perfect dessert to end a South American feast. They require only a few ingredients and are quite simple to make. The only trick when making them is to ensure you cook the fudge until thick and sticky so that they hold their shape when rolled. Aside from that just make sure you have plenty to go around as these are bound to be a hit with both young and old.

1 x 395 G (13¾ OZ) TIN CONDENSED MILK

3 TABLESPOONS UNSWEETENED COCOA POWDER

40 G (1½ OZ) BUTTER, PLUS EXTRA FOR GREASING

150 G (5 OZ) GOOD-QUALITY DARK CHOCOLATE SPRINKLES, FOR ROLLING

20 SMALL PAPER CASES

Pour the condensed milk into a small heavy-based saucepan. Sift in the cocoa, add the butter and place over medium heat, stirring occasionally, until the mixture begins to simmer. Reduce the heat to low–medium and cook for a further 10–15 minutes, stirring constantly to prevent the mixture from burning and sticking to the base of the pan. When the sauce has thickened into a very sticky fudge, spoon onto a heatproof tray and set aside for 10 minutes, to cool slightly. Refrigerate for 15 minutes, or until completely cool.

Lightly grease your hands with butter and roll 1 heaped tablespoonful of the fudge at a time to make even-sized balls. Roll each ball in chocolate sprinkles to coat and place each into a paper case. Return to the refrigerator for a further 15 minutes, or until firm but not hard.

NOTE: Brigaderios *can be made a few days in advance and stored in an airtight container in the refrigerator. Set out at room temperature for 15 minutes to soften slightly before serving.*

MAKES 20

SUSPIRO A LA LIMEÑA

PERUVIAN CARAMEL AND MERINGUE PIE

Translating as 'sigh to Lima' this Peruvian meringue is a very sweet and rich dessert that is best cut into small portions for eating — a little goes a long way! Its smooth caramel base topped with marshmallow meringue make it simply sigh-worthy.

½ CUP (125 ML/4 FL OZ) TINNED CONDENSED MILK

1 x 375 ML (12½ FL OZ) TIN EVAPORATED MILK

3 LARGE EGGS, SEPARATED

½ TEASPOON NATURAL VANILLA EXTRACT

1 CUP (220 G/8 OZ) CASTER (SUPERFINE) SUGAR

1 CUP (80 ML/3 FL OZ) PORT

GROUND CINNAMON, FOR DUSTING

To make the base of the pie, combine the condensed milk and evaporated milk in a medium-sized saucepan and bring to the boil. Reduce the heat to low and simmer for 20 minutes, stirring frequently until the mixture turns a caramel colour and thickens to coat the back of a spoon. Remove from the heat.

Place the egg yolks in a medium-sized bowl and gradually pour in the caramel milk mixture, stirring constantly to prevent the egg yolks from scrambling. Stir in the vanilla, then return the mixture to a clean saucepan over low heat and stir continuously for 3–5 minutes, or until thickened. Pour into a 20 cm (8 inch) glass pie dish or eight shallow serving glasses. Set aside.

To make the meringue topping, combine the sugar and port in a small saucepan over low heat. Stir for 3–5 minutes, or until the sugar has dissolved.

Meanwhile, using an electric mixer fitted with a whisk attachment, beat the egg whites until soft peaks form. Pour in the warm port syrup in a thin, steady stream, whisking constantly to make a thick glossy meringue. Spoon the meringue over the top of the caramel base and use a spatula or the back of a spoon to create small peaks. Lightly dust with cinnamon and refrigerate for at least 1 hour to chill and set before serving.

SERVES 8

PLÁTANOS ASADOS A LA CANELA CON HELADO DE MANGO

ROASTED CINNAMON BANANAS WITH MANGO SORBET

This is a very simple and delicious dessert to cook at the end of a barbecue meal. The sugars in the banana caramelise to create a memorably sweet soft dessert, with just a hint of spice. Served with a light and refreshing mango sorbet they are taken to another level entirely.

6 RIPE BANANAS, PEELS LEFT ON

GROUND CINNAMON, TO SERVE

MANGO SORBET

1 CUP (220 G/8 OZ) CASTER (SUPERFINE) SUGAR

3 LARGE RIPE MANGOES, PEELED, STONES
  REMOVED AND FLESH ROUGHLY CHOPPED

1 LARGE EGG WHITE, LIGHTLY BEATEN

JUICE OF 1 LIME

To make the mango sorbet, put the sugar and ¾ cup (185 ml/6½ fl oz) water in a small saucepan and gently simmer, stirring until the sugar has dissolved. Remove from the heat and set aside to cool.

Place the mango in a food processor or blender and process or blend to make a smooth purée. Transfer to a large bowl and whisk in the sugar syrup, egg white and lime juice.

Transfer to an ice cream machine and churn according to the manufacturer's instructions. Place in a large airtight container and freeze overnight.

Preheat the barbecue chargrill or hotplate to medium.

Place the bananas on the grill and cook, turning occasionally, for 5–10 minutes, or until they are completely blackened and are just beginning to split open. Transfer to a tray.

Cut the ends off the bananas and slice lengthwise to peel off the skin and open. Sprinkle with cinnamon and serve hot with a dollop of mango sorbet on the side.

SERVES 6

QUINDÃO

BRAZILIAN COCONUT BAKED CUSTARD CAKE

This rich bright yellow dessert has a sweet silky egg custard with a slightly chewy coconut base. Its high egg content of eighteen egg yolks reflects Brazil's Portuguese influence and with the addition of coconut, it's African too. It is a perfect dessert for entertaining as it can be prepared a day in advance.

18 LARGE EGG YOLKS

1½ CUPS (330 G/11½ OZ) CASTER (SUPERFINE) SUGAR, PLUS EXTRA FOR DUSTING

1½ CUPS (100 G/3½ OZ) SHREDDED COCONUT

40 G (1½ OZ) BUTTER, MELTED, PLUS EXTRA FOR GREASING

Preheat the oven to 190°C (375°F). Lightly grease a 22 cm (8½ inch) ring cake tin with the extra melted butter and dust the pan with the extra sugar.

Whisk the egg yolks and sugar together in a medium-sized bowl. Add the coconut, melted butter and 1 cup (250 ml/8½ fl oz) water and stir to combine. Pour into the prepared cake tin.

Place the tin in a deep baking tray. Set aside for 10 minutes, to allow the coconut to float to the surface — this will be the base.

Pour enough hot water into the baking tray to come halfway up the side of the tin. Bake in the oven for 50–60 minutes, or until the custard has set and the coconut top is golden brown.

Remove the tray from the oven. Carefully remove the tin and set aside for 20 minutes to cool slightly, then refrigerate until completely cool.

To serve, run a knife around the edge of the cake and use your fingertips to gently pull the cake away from the edge of the tin — this will release the seal so you can invert it onto a serving plate.

SERVES 12

DRINKS

BATIDA DE MANGO

BRAZILIAN MANGO COCKTAIL

A *batida* is essentially a blended fruit cocktail and can be made using mangoes, strawberries or a combination of mixed berries. Substitute vodka if cachaça is unavailable.

1½ CUPS (375 ML/12½ FL OZ) CACHAÇA

1.2 KG (2 LB 10 OZ) MANGO PULP, ROUGHLY CHOPPED

½ CUP (125 ML/4 FL OZ) TINNED CONDENSED MILK

¼ CUP (60 ML/2 FL OZ) LIME JUICE

4 CUPS CRUSHED ICE, PLUS EXTRA TO FILL THE JUG

Combine all of the ingredients in a blender and blend until smooth.

Transfer to a jug and top up with additional ice before pouring into individual glasses and serving.

VARIATION: To make a strawberry version, simply replace the mango pulp with 900 g (2 lb) hulled strawberries and omit the lime juice.

SERVES 10

BATIDA DE COCO

BRAZILIAN BLENDED
COCONUT COCKTAIL

This cocktail can be served in tumbler glasses with ice or served as shots for a larger crowd. Substitute vodka if cachaça is unavailable.

1½ CUPS (375 ML/12½ FL OZ) CACHAÇA

3 CUPS (750 ML/25 FL OZ) COCONUT MILK

½ CUP (125 ML/4 FL OZ) TINNED CONDENSED MILK

4 CUPS CRUSHED ICE, PLUS EXTRA TO FILL THE JUG

Combine all of the ingredients in a blender and blend until smooth.

Transfer the cocktail mixture into a jug and top up with additional ice before serving.

SERVES 10

CAIPIRINHA

BRAZILIAN CANE SUGAR
AND LIME COCKTAIL

Brazil's national drink is a cocktail that befits any barbecue or social gathering. Cachaça, pronounced 'ka-sha-sa', or *pinga*, as it is commonly referred to in Brazil, is a spirit made from fermented and distilled sugar cane juice. If you cannot find it, then a similar drink, known as a caipiroska can be made using clear, unflavoured vodka instead.

12 LIMES

½ CUP (110 G/3¾ OZ) RAW SUGAR

4 CUPS CRUSHED ICE, PLUS EXTRA TO FILL
    THE JUG

1½ CUPS (375 ML/12½ FL OZ) CACHAÇA

Cut the limes into quarters. Remove and discard the line of pith down the centre and any seeds.

Combine the limes, sugar and ice in a shaker and use a cocktail muddler or similar to pound the limes to release their flavour. Add the cachaça and shake for 10 seconds to combine. Pour into a jug to serve.

Make sure you scoop out a few lime wedges and some of the sugar into each glass before pouring.

SERVES 10

BATIDA DE ABACAXI E MARACUJÁ

BRAZILIAN BLENDED PINEAPPLE AND PASSIONFRUIT COCKTAIL

Tropical fruits are bountiful in Brazil. Colourful displays can be seen at juice bars throughout Rio de Janeiro, where they are commonly used to make vitamin-rich juices. Many of these exotic fruits are not available outside the region, however passionfruit and pineapple, both native to Brazil, are now grown in warmer regions throughout the world. Here they are blended with *cachaça* to make a refreshing jug of *batida*.

1½ CUPS (375 ML/12½ FL OZ) CACHAÇA

600 G (1 LB 5 OZ) FRESH PINEAPPLE, SKIN
    AND CORE REMOVED AND FLESH ROUGHLY
    CHOPPED

2 CUPS (500 ML/17 FL OZ) PASSIONFRUIT PULP

1–2 TABLESPOONS LIME JUICE

1½ TABLESPOONS CASTER (SUPERFINE) SUGAR

4 CUPS CRUSHED ICE, PLUS EXTRA TO FILL
    THE JUG

Combine all of the ingredients in a blender and blend until smooth.

Transfer to a jug and top up with extra crushed ice, to serve.

NOTE: You can substitute any clear unflavoured vodka if cachaça is unavailable.

SERVES 10

BATIDA DE AMENDOIM

BRAZILIAN BLENDED
PEANUT COCKTAIL

This is a very richly flavoured cocktail that is best served as shots — the peanuts and condensed milk give it a truly unique taste that is well worth trying. Substitute vodka if cachaça is unavailable.

½ CUP (80 G/3 OZ) UNSALTED PEANUTS

¼ CUP (60 ML/2 FL OZ) CACHAÇA

2 TABLESPOONS TINNED CONDENSED MILK

6 ICE CUBES, CRUSHED

Preheat the oven to 180°C (360°F).

Spread the peanuts out onto a baking tray and cook for 10–15 minutes, or until golden brown. Set aside to cool.

Once cool, transfer the peanuts to a small food processor and process to make a paste. Combine the peanut paste and the remaining ingredients in a blender and blend until smooth.

Pour into eight shot glasses, to serve.

NOTE: You can substitute ⅓ cup (80 ml/3 fl oz) freshly ground peanut butter instead of making the peanut paste if you are short on time.

SERVES 8

CLERICO

URUGUAYAN WHITE WINE SANGRIA

Packed with colourful fruits, such as orange, banana, apple, strawberries and grapes, this white wine sangria looks beautiful served in a punchbowl or large jug. It needs to be made in advance to allow the sugar and fruits to infuse and mellow the wine. It is light and refreshing and makes a lovely addition to a South American barbecue.

2 x 750 ML (25 FL OZ) BOTTLES DRY WHITE
   WINE, SUCH AS SAUVIGNON BLANC
3 CUPS (750 ML/25 FL OZ) SODA WATER
¼ CUP (50 G/2 OZ) CASTER (SUPERFINE) SUGAR
JUICE OF 2 LEMONS
2 ORANGES, PEELED, SEGMENTED AND DICED
2 BANANAS, PEELED AND SLICED
2 GREEN APPLES, QUARTERED, CORED AND
   THINLY SLICED
10 STRAWBERRIES, HULLED AND SLICED
2 CUPS (180 G/6¼ OZ) GRAPES, HALVED AND
   SEEDED
1 SMALL HANDFUL MINT LEAVES
2 CUPS CRUSHED ICE

Combine the wine, soda water, sugar and lemon juice in a large punchbowl and stir to dissolve the sugar. Add the fruit and mint, cover, and refrigerate for at least 2 hours.

Just before you are ready to serve, add the crushed ice then pour into serving glasses.

SERVES 8

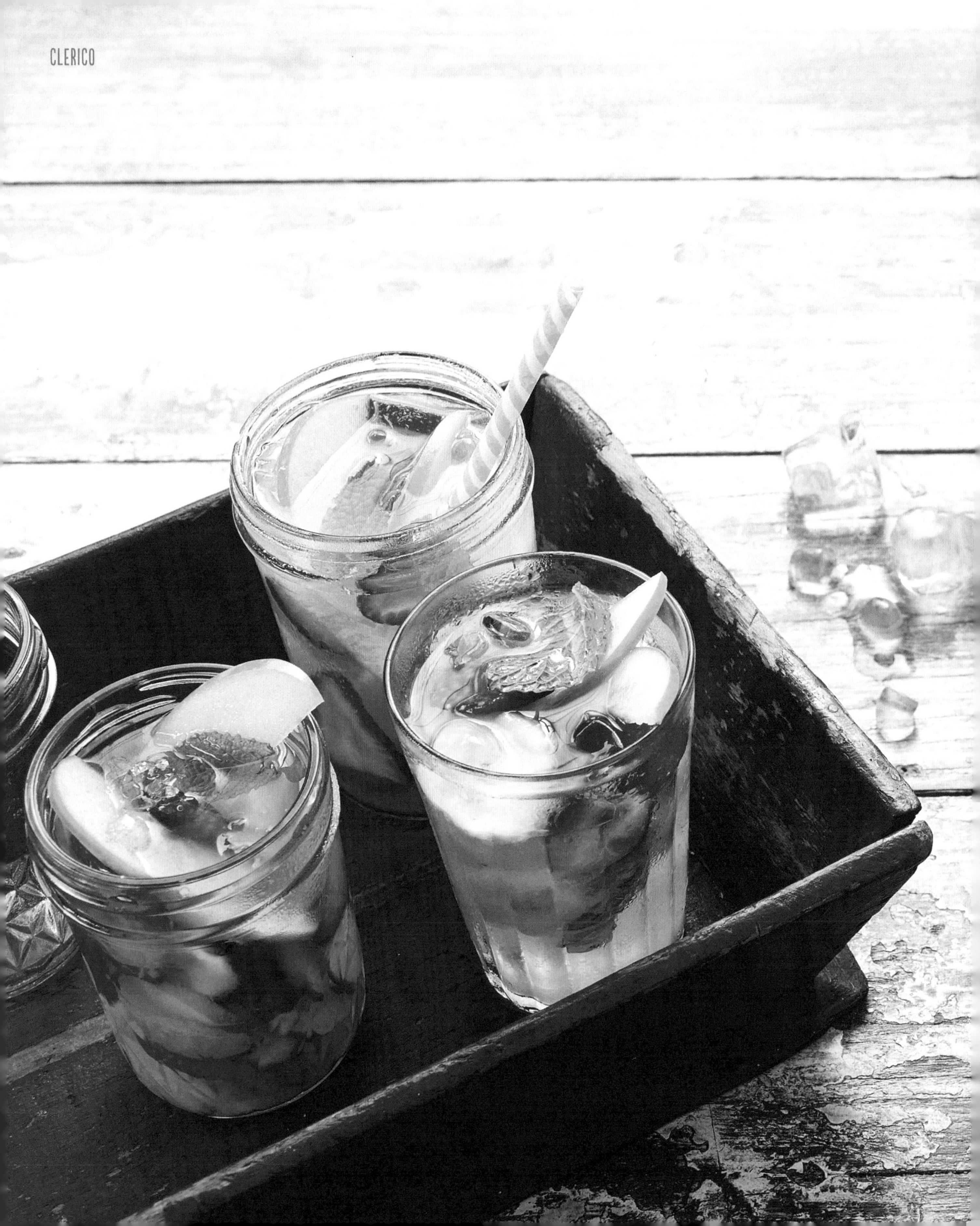

PISCO SOUR

PERUVIAN COCKTAIL

This drink is made using Pisco, a sweet brandy made from fermented grapes that is native to Peru. Pisco is available from most large bottle shops.

¼ CUP (60 ML/2 FL OZ) PISCO

2 TABLESPOONS LIME JUICE

1 LARGE EGG WHITE

6 ICE CUBES, CRUSHED

1–3 DROPS ANGOSTURA BITTERS

SUGAR SYRUP

1 CUP (220 G/8 OZ) SUGAR

1 CUP (250 ML/8 ½ FL OZ) WATER

To make the sugar syrup, combine the sugar and water in a small saucepan and gently heat for 3–5 minutes, or until the sugar has dissolved. Set aside to cool.

To make the pisco sour, combine the pisco, lime juice, egg white and 2 tablespoons of the sugar syrup in a cocktail shaker with the ice. Shake vigorously for 20–30 seconds. Pour into glasses and top with drops of bitters to serve.

NOTE: Any leftover sugar syrup can be stored in the refrigerator for up to 1 month, ensuring it is on hand for all your cocktail-making needs.

SERVES 1

INDEX

porotos granados 66

potatoes
    Brazilian potato salad 148
    Peruvian potatoes with spicy yellow
        cheese sauce 160–1
    salt-baked potatoes 128

provoleta 18

provolone, grilled, with oregano and chilli 18

pudim de leite 166

pumpkin, corn and borlotti bean stew 66

Q

quindão 185

quinoa salad 140

R

red capsicum, grilled 138

rice, Brazilian 122

rolled beef stuffed with egg and
    vegetables 72–3

rolled stuffed chicken breast 98–9

rosemary
    Argentinian grilled garlic and rosemary
        flat bread 155
    baked rosemary onions 129
    butterflied lemon and rosemary
        chicken 84–5
    garlic and rosemary oil 155
    salt-baked lamb shoulder stuffed with
        anchovy, rosemary and garlic 48–9

rotisserie abacaxi com açúcar e canela 169

rotisserie pineapple with cinnamon sugar 169

rump cap 44–5

S

salada de batatas 148

salads
    Brazilian potato salad 148
    lima bean salad 144
    palm heart salad 126

(*salads continued*)
    quinoa salad 140

salmon horneado a la sal con manteca,
    hierbas y limón 54–5

salmon, salt-baked and stuffed with herbs,
    butter and lemon 54–5

salsa criolla 110

salsa picante 100

salsas
    Brazilian salsa 115
    chilli salsa 100
    Peruvian onion salsa 110
    tomato, coriander and chilli 111

salchichas 100

salt-baked lamb shoulder stuffed with
    anchovy, rosemary and garlic 48–9

salt-baked potatoes 128

salt-baked salmon stuffed with herbs, butter
    and lemon 54–5

sandwiches
    Argentinian caramel biscuit sandwiches
        172
    grilled beef sandwich 50

sangria, Uruguayan white wine 199

sauces
    Argentinian caramel sauce 168
    Argentinian green sauce 108
    avocado sauce 114
    cheiro verde sauce 21
    chimichurri 108

sausages, South American 100

seafood
    mussels with garlic and herbs 102
    seafood coconut stew with manioc paste
        62–3

seafood, *see also* fish

sirloin, whole, roasted with *chimichurri* 42

skewers
    Brazilian fish 78
    cachaça and lime chicken 67

(*skewers continued*)
    grilled chicken drummette 35
    grilled chicken hearts 24
    grilled haloumi skewers 34
    grilled kidney skewers 14
    ox heart kebabs 38

solomillo asado con chimichurri 42

South American cuisine 6

South American sausages 100

suspiro a la limeña 180

T

tira de asado 58

tomatoes
    Brazilian salsa 115
    grilled witlof and tomato 145
    tomato, coriander and chilli salsa 111

trout, butterflied, with *vinagrete* 88

truffles, Brazilian chocolate fudge 177

truta grelhada com vinagrete 88

twice-fried plantain chips 152

U

Uruguayan white wine sangria 199

V

veal steaks, crumbed 91

Venezuelan corn parcels 132

vinagrete 115

W

witlof and tomato, grilled 145